HOMESIDE ACTIVITIES

ACTIVITIES

GRADE 1

DEVELOPMENTAL STUDIES CENTER

DEVELOPMENTAL STUDIES CENTER

2000 Embarcadero, Suite 305
Oakland, CA 94606
(510) 533-0213
(800) 666-7270

ISBN 1-885603-60-6

"The ABCs of You" by Red and Kathy
Grammer © 1991 Smilin' Atcha Music and
Red and Kathy Grammer

"March" by Elizabeth Coatsworth from
*The Random House Book of Poetry for
Children,* selected by Jack Prelutsky,
Random House, 1983.

Acknowledgments

Homeside Activities are the product of many people—thousands of parents, teachers, and children in San Ramon, Hayward, San Francisco, Cupertino, and Salinas, California; Louisville, Kentucky; Miami and Homestead, Florida; and White Plains, New York, who piloted them as part of their association over the past decade with the Child Development Project—and the staff people at Developmental Studies Center who conceived, wrote, and edited them.

Marilyn Watson, Director of the Child Development Project, has been working with these ideas for years, convinced of the many valuable ways Homeside Activities could bring parents, teachers, and children together. She and Eric Schaps, President of Developmental Studies Center, have made it possible for this work to go forward. Cindy Litman and her children Tristan, Toby, Ethan, and Rhiannon Guevin were the core of the creative team that developed these activities. Activities were also written by Marilyn Watson, Rosa Zubizaretta, Lynn Murphy, Anne Goddard, and Carolyn Hildebrandt. Sylvia Kendzior led a team of staff developers who helped teachers use the activities in their classrooms and collected feedback from them. Anne Goddard and Lynn Murphy edited the materials, Rosa Zubizarreta translated them into Spanish, and Allan Ferguson was the project's desktop publisher. Additional editorial help was provided by Ruth Holsen, Judy Weiss, and OSO Publishing Services. Art direction was by Visual Strategies and Allan Ferguson, the cover illustration by Bud Peet.

We would like to thank the following organizations for their generous support of the development of *Homeside Activities:*

The William and Flora Hewlett Foundation
The Annenberg Foundation
The Robert Wood Johnson Foundation
Anonymous Donor
Evelyn and Walter Haas, Jr. Fund

HOMESIDE ACTIVITIES

Grade 1 Teacher Pages and Activities

A Simple Parent-Teacher Partnership for Kids

No matter who you ask, you won't get an argument about whether parents should be involved in their children's education—but you won't get many suggestions for a simple, inclusive way to make it happen, either. That's why Homeside Activities are so powerful. They provide a low-key, nonthreatening way for teachers and parents to build partnerships for kids.

These short, concrete activities in English and Spanish foster communication between teachers and parents and between parents and children. They make it easy for parents to contribute a "homeside" to their children's schoolside learning. And they make it easy for children to "schedule" personal time with a parent or other caretaking adult.

Implicit in the design of Homeside Activities is a message of respect for the diversity of children's families and communities. All activities build on the value for parents and children of talking with each other and listening to each other—in their home language. The activities recognize the social capital of the relationships children go home to when the dismissal bell rings every day. It's important for children to know that the adults guiding them at home are valued by the adults guiding them at school.

Homeside Activities are introduced once or twice a month in class, completed at home, and then incorporated into a follow-up classroom activity or discussion. Typically these 15- to 20-minute activities are reciprocal parent-child interviews or opportunities to share experiences and opinions. The activities are organized by grade level, but none of them have grade-specific references; they can also be used in mixed-grade and ungraded classrooms. The activity topics relate to academic, social, or citizenship themes that are integral to the life of almost any classroom.

For example, in a "Family Folklore" activity for fifth-graders, children learn about their own history while they collect family stories at home; then they contribute to the classroom community by sharing some of these stories in class. One classroom using this activity learned about a runaway slave who lived among the Seminoles, a courtship in which a borrowed Lincoln Continental became a neighborhood attraction, and an extended-family band that serves up the entertainment for family weddings. These seemingly small pieces of information make a big difference in how children and teachers view each other in the classroom.

BENEFITS OF HOMESIDE ACTIVITIES

	FOR STUDENTS	FOR TEACHERS	FOR PARENTS

Academic/ Intellectual	• chance to "schedule" time with parent or other adult
	• build commitment to learning
	  - engage interest of parent
	  - see importance and relevance of learning to adult life
	• build literacy
	  - communicate clearly
	  - compare information
	  - compare points of view
	  - think abstractly
	• rehearse school learning
	• reinforce school learning
	• reinforce value of home language
		• students more invested in academics because of adult involvement
		• more ways to connect new learning for students
		  - more aware of students' experiences
		  - more aware of students' knowledge
		• opportunity to inform parents of classroom learning program
		• opportunity to encourage use of home language
			• fail-safe way to contribute to child's school learning
			• exposure to classroom learning approach
			• exposure to classroom learning topics
			• opportunity to enjoy child's thinking
			• opportunity to reinforce importance and relevance of learning
			• opportunity to reinforce value of home language

Citizenship	• chance to "schedule" time with parent or other adult
	• build commitment to values
	  - engage interest of parent
	  - see importance and relevance of values to adult life
	• build complex understanding of values
	  - compare information
	  - compare points of view
	  - think abstractly
	• reinforce school learning
		• students more conscious of values
		• students more open to examining their behavior
		• students more likely to see similarities between home and school values
			• exposure to citizenship focus of classroom
			• low-key way to explore child's values
			• opportunity to communicate personal values
			• more information for ongoing guidance of child

Classroom Community	• see parents as valued contributors to classroom
	• build interpersonal understanding
	  - of individuals
	  - of diverse families/situations
	• build shared learning orientation
		• more understanding and empathy
		  - for individual students
		  - for parents' hopes and concerns
		  - for diverse circumstances of students
		• more comfort inviting parents into community
		• reinforce shared learning orientation
			• more knowledge of child's classroom
			• more comfort with child's classroom
			• more comfort with child's teacher
			• opportunity to contribute to the life of the classroom
			• low-risk forum for communicating with teacher

Perhaps as important as the activity-specific information generated by Homeside Activities are the open-ended comments to teachers that parents are encouraged to write. Sometimes the remarks let the teacher in on a child's concerns, for example, about teasing or a bully; sometimes they are simply observations, such as, "Carlos loves science this year"; and sometimes they comment on the value of the activity, as in the following:

> "Allison liked this one. It got us both thinking and she shared more of the day's activities with me."

> "Tyrone says he likes doing these activities because 'your parents can help you' and because it makes you 'think about things.' I think the time spent is very special for him because we always seem to learn something about each other."

> "It was a good way to have a conversation with my son. I am grateful to you for the idea."

Of course some parents might be unable or unwilling to do the activities, in which case it may be possible to find a grandparent, older sibling, neighbor, or staff member who can be a child's regular Homeside partner. For most parents, however, as uncertain as they may be about how to help their children in school, more involvement is welcome when it is introduced through specific activities within their experience and competence. Homeside Activities provide such a structure.

The particular strengths of Homeside Activities fall into three areas: academic and intellectual, citizenship, and classroom community. The chart on page 2 shows how children, teachers, and parents can all benefit in each of these areas.

Academic and Intellectual Benefits

Homeside Activities contribute to children's academic and intellectual growth in a variety of ways—most directly by providing a motivating context for children to make connections between home and school learning. Children practice critical thinking and communication skills in every activity.

Motivates Children. Children can be expected to have a stronger investment in school and academic work if it is an investment made by their parents as well. When children have a Homeside Activity to complete, they can, in effect, schedule a parent's attention and involvement.

Includes All Parents. Because the activities engage parents around universal experiences—of growing up, of having opinions, of having adult perspectives on things children are learning—the activities are inclusive and no parent need feel intimidated or incapable of contributing.

"It was a good way to have a conversation with my son."

Values Home Languages. For families whose home language is not English, the activities send the message that the school values communication in the home language. For Spanish-speakers this message is explicit since the activities are available in Spanish. For those with home languages other than Spanish or English, students will have gone over the activities in class and will be prepared to serve as "activity directors" at home.

Promotes Literacy and Thinking Skills. In doing these activities children practice literacy and thinking skills of talking, listening, synthesizing information to report to parents or back to the classroom, and comparing and evaluating information and points of view—skills that are core competencies for academic and life success.

Educates Parents about a "Thinking" Curriculum. Many parents were educated at a time when memorization and rote learning were the primary goals of schooling. Homeside Activities can introduce these parents to a "thinking" curriculum that asks open-ended questions and encourages problem solving and divergent thinking. Rather than limiting parents' role to one of monitoring homework completion, for example, Homeside Activities invite parents to participate in their children's learning experiences and allow them to enjoy their children's ideas and thought processes.

Makes Children's Past Experiences and Prior Knowledge More Accessible to the Teacher. Homeside Activities bring new areas of children's experience into the classroom, broadening the possible connections teachers can help children make when they are constructing new knowledge. When teachers and children have widely different background experiences, this can be especially important.

> Children practice critical thinking and communication skills in every activity

Citizenship Benefits

Many Homeside Activities involve children and parents in discussions of ethical behavior and principled choices about how to treat oneself and others. The activities provide parents and children with a comfortable way to exchange ideas about important values in their family.

Deepens Children's Ethical Commitment. When ethical concerns such as ways we treat a friend or how we identify "heroes" are raised at school and reinforced at home, children see their parents and teachers as partners for their ethical development. Children respond positively when the most important adults in their lives demonstrate congruent investment in their growth as kind and principled human beings.

Strengthens Children's Development as Decision Makers. The time children spend thinking about and discussing citizenship goals and ethical concerns helps them build complex understanding of these issues and prepares them to become autonomous, ethical decision makers. Homeside Activities provide a way for children to anticipate ethical choices and rehearse future behaviors.

Enhances Parental Guidance. When parents and children can exchange ideas about citizenship goals and ethical concerns in the context of Homeside Activities, rather than in response to an immediate problem, the discussion can be less loaded for both. In such a context, children may be more likely to let parents into their sometimes mysterious world, and parents may welcome a conversational approach for transmitting their values.

Classroom Community Benefits

Homeside Activities structure a way to build children's and parents' personal connections to the classroom—to create a shared feeling of community.

Invites Parents into the Community. Homeside Activities are invitations to parents to learn more about the life of their children's classroom. They are also a way for parents to become comfortable communicating with their children's teacher.

Encourages Parents to Contribute Directly to the Life of the Classroom. Information that parents contribute to the classroom through Homeside Activities deepens students' understanding of each other, provides teachers with insights into children's diverse family situations, and models the school's respect for the home cultures and family experiences of all students. At the same time, Homeside Activities do not require parents who are too busy, too tired, or too embarrassed to be anyplace other than at home with their child when making their contributions.

Reinforces a Learning Orientation. A classroom community is defined by the shared goals of its members. Homeside Activities, by virtue of their content and approach, make it clear to everyone involved with the classroom that its members are learning about learning, learning about ethical behavior, and learning about how to treat one another respectfully.

How These Activities Were Developed

Homeside Activities have been piloted and field-tested in the hundreds of classrooms across the country that have participated in the Child Development Project (CDP), a comprehensive school change effort to help elementary schools become inclusive, caring communities and stimulating, supportive places to learn. Our research has identified several conditions that children need to reach their fullest social and academic potential:

- close and caring relationships with their peers and teachers;
- opportunities to practice and benefit from prosocial values;
- compelling, relevant curriculum; and
- close cooperation and communication between families and school.

> A comfortable way to exchange ideas about important values

Homeside Activities are one of the many approaches CDP has developed to meet these conditions, and over the past decade that the Homeside Activities have been used in CDP schools, we have discovered many ways to make them easier for teachers to justify academically, easier for *all* parents to respond to, and "friendlier" for kids to bring home.

FIELD-TEST FEEDBACK

Feedback from teachers, parents, and students about all aspects of Homeside Activities, coupled with our own classroom and home observations, led us to strengthen and highlight many aspects of the program, especially the following:

1. Provide teachers with introductory and follow-up classroom activities that help them incorporate the Homeside Activities into their academic programs.

2. Make the academic relevance of the activities clear to parents.

3. Make no demands in the activities that might require any resources that could exclude parents from participating.

4. Streamline the amount of information provided to parents, and use simple vocabulary and syntax.

5. Make clear that the activities are voluntary and should be enjoyable.

6. Make clear that the activities are open-ended and not "tests" of children's academic performance or ability.

7. Emphasize the importance of not grading the activities or penalizing students who are unable to return them.

8. Allow at least a week for completion of the activities.

9. Represent diverse cultures in the activity poems, quotes, songs, and other references.

10. Screen all activities for cultural sensitivity.

Guidelines for Teachers

All Homeside Activities are built around parent-child conversations and usually involve students in a short drawing or writing activity. The activities for grades K–3 are addressed to adults, and adults direct the conversation; the activities for grades 4–5 are addressed to students and are student-directed. To increase both parents' and children's comfort and success in using the activities, consider the following guidelines.

Introduce the Activities Early in the Year. During back-to-school night or a similar beginning-of-the-year occasion, personally and enthusiastically inform parents about the purpose and benefits of Homeside Activities—this definitely enhances parents' responsiveness when their children begin bringing home these assignments. If you use the first Homeside Activity in your grade-level set, "Introducing Homeside Activities," it also explains the nature of these assignments. In addition to or instead of "Introducing Homeside Activities," you might send a letter to your students' parents to explain your goals for the activities (see, for example, "A Note about Homeside Activities" on page 9). And as new children enroll in your class, be sure to communicate with their parents about your Homeside Activities program.

Explain What the Activities Are and What They Are Not. Most parents appreciate these activities and enjoy the time spent with their children, but you may also meet with some resistance from parents who misunderstand them. To preclude some possible objections, it is important to present the activities in such a way that they don't appear to be a prescription for "fixing" families or for teaching parents how to communicate with their children. Be prepared to speak with parents who expect traditional homework assignments: some may need to understand that this is "real" homework, because conversation is as important to their child's development as are other assignments. Above all, emphasize that these are supposed to be enjoyable, not a burden to either the parents or the children.

Encourage Parents to Use Their Home Language. Be sure parents understand that it's perfectly fine for them to do these activities in their home language. Point out the value to their children of developing facility in their home language as well as in English.

Use Homeside Activities Often. To see that these assignments are viewed neither as a burden nor a novelty, use them frequently enough for parents and students to see them as an integral part of the classroom program (ideally, one or two times per month). When scheduling their use, keep in mind two considerations: allow families one full week to complete each activity, preferably including a weekend; also coordinate with other teachers so that a family isn't inundated by having all their children bring these activities home at the same time.

Adjust Your Own Homework Habits. Make it clear to students (as well as their parents) that these Homeside Activities do not increase their homework load, but are part of it. This may mean that you have to adjust your own homework plans so that these activities are assigned instead of, rather than in addition to, a typical assignment.

Help Students Engage Family Members. Treat Homeside Activities with the same seriousness you use for other homework, but do not penalize students when circumstances beyond their control make it impossible or counterproductive to complete an activity. If possible, help students find ways around obstacles they may encounter; when a parent is not available, for example,

Homeside Activities link children's school and home lives

encourage students to enlist the participation of other older family members or other older people. You might also have students brainstorm ways to encourage their family's participation, such as thinking ahead to when might be the best time to introduce an activity—not, for example, the night before the assignment is due, or as parents are rushing to get to work or to get dinner on the table.

Review or Rehearse the Activities in Class. All the activities are accompanied by ideas for introducing them in class and reviewing what it is that students will be doing at home. Students will feel more confident doing Homeside Activities when they have had a chance to practice or review them first. For example, when the activity asks students to interview their parents, you might have them first ask you or a partner the interview questions. In this way, students will already have an idea of what to say when they begin their dialogue with their parents; also, if their parents are not proficient in English, then the children will "know" how the assignment is supposed to go and can help their parents carry it out. Also, many teachers report that previewing the activity "jump-starts" students' enthusiasm for doing it at home.

Have Fun! Again, in considering these guidelines and planning a program of Homeside Activities, remember that flexibility and fun are key to making them work. No one needs to look for the "right" answers to questions, for the "right" conversation to take place, for the "right" products to be returned to class. Instead, the purpose and benefits of Homeside Activities are broader and perhaps more ambitious: to encourage family interactions that link children's school and home lives. We hope you will enjoy these rewarding connections among school, home, students, parents, and teachers.

Dear Family Members and Family Friends,

Welcome to Homeside Activities! Your child will bring these home to do with you once or twice a month—to add a "homeside" to the "schoolside" learning we are doing in class. These 15- to 20-minute activities

- are built around conversations between you and your child,
- deal with topics and ideas related to your child's schoolwork;
- may involve your child in a short writing or drawing activity, and
- help create a partnership between school and home.

You will find that in Homeside Activities there are no "right" or "wrong" answers, no right or wrong ways to do the activities. You can take the conversation in any direction you want, and you can have as many family members participate as you'd like. Just having these conversations is what counts, because they help your child develop thinking and language skills for life. These assignments contribute to your child's academic and social learning because

- they help you stay in touch with your child's learning;
- working with you increases your child's interest in the work;
- your child gets to practice communication skills and think about important ideas; and
- your child learns from you and sees how school learning relates to "real life."

These don't take long to do, and I'll try to give you plenty of time to fit them into your schedule. Also, teachers will plan together when to use these activities. That way, if you have several children at school, they won't all bring these home at the same time.

Thanks for taking the time to share these wonderful learning experiences with us. I hope you and your child enjoy Homeside Activities.

Your child's teacher,

Estimados padres, familiares y amigos:

¡Bienvenidos a las Actividades Familiares! Su hija o su hijo traerá estas actividades a casa una o dos veces al mes, para realizarlas junto con Uds. Esto le añadirá una dimensión hogareña a nuestro aprendizaje escolar. Cada actividad requiere de 15 a 20 minutos. En su conjunto, las actividades

- reconocen la importancia fundamental del diálogo familiar;
- tratan ideas y temas relacionados al trabajo escolar de su hija o de su hijo;
- con frecuencia incluyen una breve actividad de dibujo o de escritura y
- ayudan a crear una mejor colaboración entre la escuela y el hogar.

Encontrará que no hay respuestas "correctas" ni "incorrectas" a las Actividades Familiares, ni tampoco maneras correctas o incorrectas de llevarlas a cabo. Puede orientar el diálogo en la dirección que guste, y solicitar la participación de todos los miembros de la familia que desee. Lo importante es el simple hecho de tener estas conversaciones en el idioma que Ud. domina, ya que ésa es la mejor manera de guiar a su hija o a su hijo y de ayudarle a desarrollar su capacidad de razonar. Si su hija o su hijo aprende a comunicarse bien en el idioma del hogar, esto le ayudará a dominar con mayor facilidad el idioma de la escuela. Y el hablar bien dos idiomas le será una gran ventaja a lo largo de su vida.

Estas tareas familiares apoyan el aprendizaje académico y social , ya que:

- le ayudan a Ud. a estar al tanto de lo que su hija o su hijo está aprendiendo en la escuela;
- el trabajar con Ud. despierta el interés de su hija o de su hijo por los trabajos escolares;
- su hija o su hijo puede ejercer sus habilidades de comunicación y pensar acerca de ideas significativas;
- su hija o su hijo aprende de Ud., y puede darse cuenta de cómo lo que aprende en la escuela se relaciona con la vida cotidiana.

Las actividades no le llevarán demasiado tiempo, y trataré de darles un buen plazo en el cual las podrán cumplir. Las maestras también coordinarán el uso de las actividades entre sí, para evitar que, si usted tiene varios niños en la misma escuela, todos le traigan actividades a casa a la misma vez.

Le agradezco el que se tome el trabajo de compartir estos valiosos momentos de aprendizaje con nosotros. Espero que disfruten las Actividades Familiares.

Atentamente,

Introducing Homeside Activities

Before Sending Home the Activity

Introduce students to Homeside Activities and have a class discussion about how they are different from other homework assignments. Ask students to talk with a partner about what they think they will enjoy about doing Homeside Activities with a parent or adult friend, and what might be hard about doing Homeside Activities.

Have students design covers for Homeside Activity folders on manila folders or envelopes. Send the folders home with the first Homeside Activity. Have students keep completed Homeside Activities in their folders, until they bring the folders and completed activities home again with the final Homeside Activity of the year.

Follow-Up

Have students share their reactions to the first Homeside Activity. What did they enjoy about the activity? What did their parent or adult friend enjoy? What problems did students encounter? What was most interesting about the activity? Most surprising? Give students a chance to show and explain their pictures to their partners or to the class.

Introducing Homeside Activities

Dear Family Member or Family Friend,

This year I will be sending home some Homeside Activities. These ask your child to talk with a parent or other adult about topics related to our classroom work. Each Homeside Activity includes a brief explanation and some questions or ideas to help you and your child do the activity. Most of them also ask your child to draw or write about doing the activity. There is no "correct" way to do these Homeside Activities, except to just enjoy them together. They are a way to recognize and value how much you can teach your child, by sharing your thoughts and experiences with him or her.

For this first Homeside Activity, your child will show you a folder he or she made to hold the activities through the year. Please use the Conversation Starters to talk about the Homeside Activities. Then ask your child to draw a picture about your conversation on the back of this page.

Thanks for your time, and have fun!

Conversation Starters

Ask your child to show you his or her Homeside Activities folder. Then use the questions below to talk about the folder and about Homeside Activities. You can also add your own questions. But don't worry about writing down your child's answers—I want children to practice their *talking* skills!

1 Tell me about the folder and how you designed it. What do you think the Homeside Activities will be like? How will they be different from other kinds of homework?

2 What topics do you like to talk with adults about? Are there adults at school or in the community that you enjoy talking to? Why?

3 Now tell your child about a parent or other adult whom you enjoyed talking to when you were a child. Ask your child to draw a picture of you talking to that person when you were a child.

In the space below, have your child draw a picture of you talking to the adult you told your child about. If you'd like, help your child write a caption for the picture.

Comments

After you have completed this activity, each of you please sign your name and the date below. If you have any comments, please write them in the space provided.

Signatures   Date

Please have your child return this activity to school. Thank you.

Starting School!

Before Sending Home the Activity

As this is one of the first Homeside Activities that you'll be using with your students, it's particularly important that you go over it with them before they take it home. For example, to get students into the spirit of the activity, you might lead them in a visualization exercise after you have explained the assignment: Have them take a good look around the classroom and then close their eyes; ask them to describe different parts of the room with their eyes closed.

Follow-Up

Set some time aside for a class "show-and-tell," giving students a chance to show and explain their drawings to their classmates; this could also lead to a discussion of what your students want to learn this year, why they prefer certain subjects, and the like.

Starting School!

Dear Family Member or Family Friend,

The start of the school year is exciting and sometimes a little scary for children. Of course, we want to encourage their eagerness about what lies ahead. In class, we've been spending time getting to know each other, learning the rules of the classroom, and talking about some of the things we'll be doing this year.

For this activity, please use the Conversation Starters to talk with your child about this new school year. Your child may have told you about some of this already, so you can ask your own questions, too. Then on the back of this page have your child draw a picture of himself or herself learning about something really interesting. From this activity, you'll know more about our classroom, and I'll get to know your child better.

Thanks for your time, and have fun!

Conversation Starters

Here are some questions you might ask your child to get your conversation started. You can also make up different questions. You don't need to write down answers—I want children to practice their *talking* skills!

1 Tell me about your classroom. What do you like about the classroom? What books or equipment do you want to use?

2 Tell me about a friend you have made in class. Why are you friends? Who else might become a good friend? Why?

3 What do you like best about your new class?

4 What do you want to learn this year? Why do you think this will be interesting?

In the space below, have your child draw a picture of himself or herself learning something interesting in school. If you'd like, help your child write a caption for the picture.

Comments

After you have completed this activity, each of you please sign your name and the date below. If you have any comments, please write them in the space provided.

Signatures   **Date**

Please have your child return this activity to school. Thank you.

Philipok

Before Sending Home the Activity

It might be a good idea to tell the story of Philipok to your students before you send the activity home, in case the person who reads the story out loud at home is not fluent in English or Spanish or has difficulty reading. This way, children already will be familiar with the story and will be somewhat prepared to think about the activity questions. You might also want to get students interested in the activity by comparing your early school experience to Philipok's, telling how you felt about going to school and what you liked to learn.

Follow-Up

One of the central issues in this story is that of Philipok's disobedience—is it sometimes okay to disobey? Do people sometimes disobey without thinking, without meaning to be "bad"? It might make for an interesting class discussion to refer to the first question in the Conversation Starters, leading the students to talk about why it's important to think about parents' reasons for asking you to do (or not do) things—and why Philipok lost sight of that in his eagerness to go to school.

Philipok

by Leo Tolstoy

There once was a boy named Philip. Because he was still so small, everyone called him Philipok. One day when his brothers and sisters were leaving for school he put on his cap and started to go with them. But his mother said:

"Where are you off to, Philipok?"

"To school."

"You're still too young for school, Philipok. You must stay home."

The older children left. Their father had gone early that morning to his job in the forest. Now their mother left to do housework for a wealthy neighbor. Philipok remained alone with his grandmother.

The grandmother was very old; as usual, she was now asleep in the corner over the stove. Philipok was lonesome and bored. He looked for his cap. He couldn't find it. He put on his father's old one and set out for school by himself.

The schoolhouse was at the far end of the village, near the church. When Philipok walked down his own street, the dogs didn't bother him—they knew him. But later, as he was passing the houses of strangers, several dogs rushed out at him from their yards. One of them was huge. They were all running after him and barking. Philipok ran away. The dogs ran after him, barking harder than ever. Philipok screamed, stumbled, and fell.

A man came out, chased the dogs away, and said to the little boy, "Where are you going all by yourself, little one?"

Philipok didn't answer him, but lifted the sides of his long coat and ran as fast as his legs would carry him. He ran all the way to the schoolhouse. There was no one in sight on the porch, but he could hear the voices of the children reading their lessons out loud inside the schoolroom. Philipok felt scared. "What if teacher chases me away?" he thought. He didn't know what to do now. If he went back home, he'd be chased by those dogs. But he was also afraid of the teacher.

Just then a woman carrying a pail of water walked past the school. She saw Philipok and said to him, "The other children are inside, learning. Why are you wasting your time out here?"

Philipok went inside. He removed his cap in the hall and opened the door to the schoolroom. It was full of children. They were talking and shouting. The teacher, wearing a red muffler, was pacing up and down between the rows of tables.

"What do you want?" he asked Philipok in a stern voice.

The little boy clutched his cap and said nothing.

"Who are you?"

He kept silent.

"Have you lost your tongue?"

Philipok was so frightened by now that he couldn't utter a word.

"Go on home if you don't want to speak," the teacher said.

The little boy would have gladly said something, but his throat was dry from fright. He stared at the teacher and began to cry. The teacher felt sorry for Philipok. He patted his head and asked the children who he was.

The children cried, "It's Philipok, Kostushkin's little brother." "He always begs to go to school." "His mother wouldn't let him." "Now he has come on the sly."

"In that case, little one, go sit down on that bench, next to your brother. I'm going to ask your mother to let you come to school from now on," the teacher said.

Then he began to show Philipok his ABCs, but the little boy already knew all the letters. He could even read a little.

"Now tell me how you spell your name," said the teacher.

Looking down bashfully at his feet and stammering, Philipok hastily spelled his name, as if he were afraid that the letters would run away if he didn't hurry.

The class burst out laughing.

"Good boy!" said the teacher. "Tell me, who taught you all this?"

Feeling bolder now, Philipok blurted out, "My brother Kostushka. I am a clever one, I learn fast. I am terribly smart!"

The teacher laughed and said, "Don't be in such a hurry to sing your own praises. Study a while first."

From that day on, Philipok came to school with his brothers and sisters.

Philipok

Dear Family Member or Family Friend,

Today I'm sending home a story for you to read to your child. The story was written by Leo Tolstoy, the great Russian novelist. Many people don't know that Tolstoy wrote stories for children, as well as for adults.

This tale is about a boy who wants to go to school, even though some people think he's too young. It's a good story for early in the school year, when children are getting used to being back in school.

Please read the story of Philipok to your child. Then use the Conversation Starters to help your child think about the story and about what he or she would like to learn this year. After your conversation, have your child draw a picture about the story on the back of this page.

Thanks for your time, and have fun!

Conversation Starters

Here are some questions you might ask your child to get your conversation started. You can also make up different questions. You don't need to write down answers—I want children to practice their *talking* skills!

1 What do you think about Philipok going to school without his mother's permission?

2 Why do you think Philipok wanted to go to school? Why else would someone want to go to school?

3 Philipok was very good at spelling his own name. He could even read a little. What are some of the things you are good at in school (such as the alphabet, counting, reading your name, drawing, singing, games)?

4 Philipok wanted to learn new things at school. What are some things you would like to learn this year? Why will this be interesting?

5 If you'd like, tell your child a memory of your own about going to school when you were a child. Were you eager, like Philipok? Was it ever scary for you? Then have your child draw a picture about Philipok on the back of this page.

In the space below, have your child draw a picture of something that happened in the story of Philipok. If you'd like, help your child write a caption for the picture.

Comments

After you have completed this activity, each of you please sign your name and the date below. If you have any comments, please write them in the space provided.

Signatures

Date

Please have your child return this activity to school. Thank you.

What Is Easy

Before Sending Home the Activity

Engage children in a discussion about things that are easy and difficult to do. You might want to get their thinking started by sharing some personal examples. Ask children if there are things that their older brothers or sisters, or their parents, are able to do that they would like to be able to do, but that are too difficult for them now. Ask what things children can do easily right now that they couldn't do when they were younger.

Using the children's examples of easy and difficult tasks, ask for their ideas about the different ways that difficult things might become easy. Try to avoid competitive comparisons of ability among students by emphasizing that everyone—including grown-ups—finds some things easy and some things difficult throughout their lives. Students might find it interesting to see that some things become easier because we work at them, and others only become easier when we get bigger or stronger.

Follow-Up

Have a class discussion about the things children have listed as "hard." Talk about how those things might become less "hard."

What Is Easy

Dear Family Member or Family Friend,

Young children must learn many new things, both in and out of school. Sometimes they get discouraged because they have a hard time doing some things that are easy for an older brother or sister or a parent. We hope that this Homeside Activity will help your child see that he or she has learned to do many things that once seemed hard, and that many things that now seem hard will someday be easy.

As you and your child make lists of things that each of you finds easy and difficult to do, your child will see that adults as well as children find some things hard to do.

Thanks for your time, and have fun!

Conversation Starters

Here are some questions you might ask your child to get your conversation started. You can also make up different questions.

1 Ask your child the following questions. On the back of this page, list the things your child mentions.

- What things can you think of that are easy for you to do right now?

- What things are hard for you to do?

2 Tell your child about some activities that are easy for you and some that are difficult. List these on the back of this page.

3 Look at your child's "easy" list and ask if all the items would have been on the "easy" list one year ago. Tell your child about how some of the things on your "easy" list got there.

4 Look at your child's "hard" list and ask if he or she thinks any of those things will ever be easy to do. Ask which of the "hard" things your child would like to be able to do, and share some ideas about ways those hard things might get easier.

5 Tell your child some ideas you have to make an item on your "hard" list easier, and ask the child for ideas that might help you.

What is easy for the child

....

....

....

....

What is hard for the child

....

....

....

....

What is easy for the adult

....

....

....

....

What is hard for the adult

....

....

....

....

Comments

After you have completed this activity, each of you please sign your name and the date below. If you have any comments, please write them in the space provided.

....

....

....

....

....

Signatures   **Date**

....

Please have your child return this activity to school. Thank you.

Alphabet Game

Before Sending Home the Activity

Explain the game to the class. Then have students practice the game with a partner, or do the first several letters of the alphabet as a class.

Follow-Up

Have partners show each other and discuss what they have written on their Homeside Activity sheet. Then survey the class about which letters were the hardest and easiest to find. Keep a tally on the board. Ask for students' speculations about why some letters might be harder to find than others.

Alphabet Game

Dear Family Member or Family Friend,

In class we are doing many activities using the letters of the alphabet. When children begin to learn the alphabet, they enjoy recognizing letters all around them. This activity is one way for children to have fun using their new knowledge.

For this activity, please follow the Game Instructions to play a letter-finding game with your child. You can play this at home or on a walk through your neighborhood, and you can also include other family members. Please play the game together, not competitively—it is important for children to know that people help each other learn and that learning can be fun!

Thanks for your time, and enjoy the game.

Game Instructions

1 With your child, find the letter "A" somewhere in the house (or outdoors). For example, you could look at books, newspapers, food containers, clothing labels, mailboxes, signs, posters, billboards, and so on. Then look for the next letter in the alphabet. Continue in this manner for as long as you are enjoying it. (Remember that it's a game, and we want it to be fun!)

For a variation, you could give yourselves a time limit to find each letter as many times as possible (in five minutes, for example).

2 Talk with your child about the game. Help him or her write answers to the questions on the back of this page.

Which were the hardest letters to find? (List as many as you'd like.)

Which were the easiest letters to find? (List as many as you'd like.)

Comments

After you have completed this activity, each of you please sign your name and the date below. If you have any comments, please write them in the space provided.

Signatures   **Date**

Please have your child return this activity to school. Thank you.

Neighborhood Walk

Before Sending Home the Activity

As it might be hard for children to get the idea of taking a walk without talking to their companions, it might be a good idea to try this activity out in the classroom first. For example, you could

- have your students, in pairs, form a circle around the outside of the classroom;

- have all the pairs take a turn around the room without talking, making mental notes of what they find most interesting; and then

- have them talk about their observations, first with each other and then as a class.

You also could plan with another teacher to send this activity home at the same time, so that beforehand your classes could do the "observation walk" in each other's classrooms to give the students something less familiar to look at.

Follow-Up

This activity would be suitable for a partner interview follow-up or a whole-class "show and tell" of students' pictures.

Neighborhood Walk

Dear Family Member or Family Friend,

In class this year we will spend some time trying to understand the world around us by "seeing" things from other people's points of view. Since we all see things in slightly different ways—we like different songs, different landscapes, different books, different food—appreciating such differences becomes an important part of growing up.

For this activity, you and your child will see a small piece of the world through each other's eyes. To do so, you will need to do this: First, take a short walk in your neighborhood together. Try to look at things carefully along the way, but don't talk to each other about what you see. Then when you get home, tell each other the five most interesting things you saw, and list them in the space provided.

After you have made your lists, use the Conversation Starters to compare your observations. You might even want to take the walk again, so you can get to see what the other person saw! On the back of this page, have your child draw something interesting one of you saw on the walk.

Thanks for your time, and have fun!

The Most Interesting Things

In the spaces below, write the five most interesting things that each of you saw on the walk. (It's OK if some of the things are the same.)

Child's Point of View

....

....

....

....

....

Adult's Point of View

....

....

....

....

....

Conversation Starters

1 Ask what your child was thinking about during the walk. Then tell what you were thinking. How were your thoughts alike or different? Why was this so?

2 How did it feel to walk without being able to talk to each other? What do you think the reason was for not talking?

3 Did you both think some of the same things were interesting, or different things? Why? What does this mean about how you each see the world?

In the space below, have your child draw a picture of something interesting that one of you saw on the walk. If you'd like, help your child write a caption for the picture.

Comments

After you have completed this activity, each of you please sign your name and the date below. If you have any comments, please write them in the space provided.

....

....

....

....

....

Signatures   Date

Please have your child return this activity to school. Thank you.

The Sorting Game

Before Sending Home the Activity

If your class has not done sorting and classifying yet, begin some sorting and classifying activities a week or so before sending the activity home. On the day you send the activity home, go over the instructions on the Homeside Activity page. You may want to demonstrate the game by playing it with a student volunteer and using classroom objects.

Follow-Up

Ask students what they thought of the activity and what were some of the hardest categorization decisions they had to make. Students may enjoy playing the game again in class with partners.

The Sorting Game

Dear Family Member or Family Friend,

O ur class is learning about classifying and sorting. We are learning that objects can be sorted in many different ways, depending on what we observe about them and what we think they have in common.

For this activity, you and your child will work together to think of different ways you might sort ten household items. Please use the Game Directions to play the "Sorting Game." There are no "right" or "wrong" answers in this activity—the point is to encourage your child to think about a variety of ways to solve the problem and to have fun together.

Thanks for your time, and enjoy the activity!

Game Directions

1 Gather ten different household items (for example, an apple, a banana, a carton of milk, a bean, a box of cereal, a paper towel, a toy car, a tube of toothpaste, an envelope, and a newspaper).

2 With your child, think of different ways to sort the items into two groups (for example, small/large, can be eaten/cannot be eaten, flat/not flat, bright/dull, red/not red, belongs in a drawer/does not belong in a drawer, and so on).

3 Choose one way to group the items and together decide which group to put each item in. Some things may be hard to classify. For example, can toothpaste be eaten, or not? Is the newspaper flat or not flat? Is your ripe banana bright or dull? It doesn't matter which group you decide to put an item in—what is important is discussing the thinking behind your decision.

4 On the back of this page, have your child draw a picture of the two groups of objects.

5 Ask your child to choose a second way to group the same objects and repeat step 3. Keep repeating the activity, using different groupings, for as long as you are enjoying yourselves. If you want, you can invite other family members to play.

Have your child draw a picture of the objects after you have sorted them into two groups. Help your child label each group to show how the objects were classified.

Comments

After you have completed this activity, each of you please sign your name and the date below. If you have any comments, please write them in the space provided.

Signatures

Date

Please have your child return this activity to school. Thank you.

The Story of My Name

Before Sending Home the Activity

After a brief discussion of what names mean—why we have them, what purpose they serve, and so on—describe the activity and model it by telling the story of how you were named. The following books tie in nicely with this activity:

- *But Names Will Never Hurt Me,* by Bernard Waber, in which Alison Wonderland learns how her parents came to choose her name; and

- *The Other Emily,* by Gibbs Davis, in which Emily discovers that she is still special, even though another girl in her class has the same name.

- *No volvais a llamarme "conejito mío,"* by Grégoire Solotareff, tells the story of Johnny Carrot, who becomes very upset when everyone calls him "my dear little rabbit" instead of using his real name.

- *Tianguis de nombres,* by Gilberto Rendón Ortiz, tells the story of an enterprising critter who creates a booming business selling new and elegant names to her insect friends, until at last they realize the true value of their own names.

Follow-Up

After volunteers have told the class the stories of their names, make a bulletin board display with their drawings.

The Story of My Name

Dear Family Member or Family Friend,

Does your child know the story of how he or she was named? In class we will be making a bulletin board showing the stories of our names.

For this activity, tell everything you can remember about how you chose your child's name. The Conversation Starters might help you remember some details. If your child already knows this story, let him or her tell it to you. Then have your child draw a picture about this story. We will share some of these stories, and our drawings, in class.

Thanks for your time, and have fun!

Conversation Starters

If it's helpful, use these ideas to get you started in telling the story.

1 Tell everything you can remember about choosing your child's name, including a middle name.

- Was it easy to choose a name?
- How long did it take?
- Who gave suggestions?
- Did you name your child after a relative? A friend? An admired person or hero?
- What would you have named your child if he had been a girl/she had been a boy?

2 Tell your child what you know about how you were named.

3 Tell your child how you felt about your own first name when you were her or his age. Then have your child draw a picture about the story of his or her name on the back of this page.

In the space below, have your child draw a picture about the story of his or her name. If you'd like, help your child write a caption for the picture.

Comments

After you have completed this activity, each of you please sign your name and the date below. If you have any comments, please write them in the space provided.

Signatures

Date

Please have your child return this activity to school. Thank you.

Talking Pictures

Before Sending Home the Activity

As a class, practice creating stories from pictures. Give students a variety of magazines from which to choose pictures for the Homeside Activity, and have them mount their pictures on construction paper for transporting home and back.

Follow-Up

Give students a chance to tell each other about doing the activity at home, either in pairs or in a class discussion.

Talking Pictures

Dear Family Member or Family Friend,

In school, children often draw pictures to illustrate stories. For this activity, though, your child will do just the opposite and make up a story about a picture. Your child has chosen a magazine picture to tell you about; if you'd like, you can use the Conversation Starters to help begin talking about it.

Creating a story from a picture helps improve your child's observation and communication skills, but you don't have to take the assignment too seriously—the main point is to use your imaginations and to have fun!

Thanks for your time, and enjoy your conversation.

Conversation Starters

Below are some questions and ideas to use in your conversation with your child. You can also make up different questions. You don't need to write down your child's answers—I want children to practice their *talking* skills!

1 Talk with your child about the magazine picture he or she brought home from school. For example, you might ask:

- Why did you choose this picture?
- What is the most interesting thing about it?
- How does it make you feel?

2 Describe your own observations, thoughts, and feelings about the picture.

3 Ask your child to make up a story about the picture. The story can be simple. For example, it might just describe what your child thinks is happening in the picture.

4 Ask your child to write a title for the story on the back of this page.

In the space below, have your child write a title for his or her story.
(You may help your child with the writing.)

The title of my story

_____

....

_____

....

_____

....

_____

....

_____

....

Comments
....
After you have completed
this activity, each of you
please sign your name and
the date below. If you have
any comments, please
write them in the space
provided.

Signatures

Date

_____

Please have your child return this activity to school. Thank you.

The ABCs of You

Before Sending Home the Activity

Read the lyrics (or play a recording) of "The ABCs of You." Give students a chance to ask about words they don't know. (Make sure students know that it isn't necessary, or even expected, that they understand all the words.)

For your Spanish-speaking students, you may want to explain that the Spanish poem is not a direct translation of the English poem, but rather a re-creation that uses different words but a similar structure. Again, not all of the words will be familiar to students, but the overall meaning is clear.

Follow-Up

Give students a chance to talk about doing the activity and to tell the class (or a partner) about their lists.

Students may enjoy working individually, with partners, or as a class to do one or more of the following:

- generate their own ABCs for a subject of their choice

- pick the lyrics that are most interesting, funniest, weirdest, most difficult, and so on

- find a word they would like to learn more about, and then do it

- pick a favorite word and use it at least five times today

- make up their own activity for "The ABCs of You"

The ABCs of You

Dear Family Member or Family Friend,

This song is made up of words beginning with all the letters of the alphabet. For this activity, please read aloud the lyrics with your child. (Your child won't know what all the words in the song mean. Explain any that your child asks about, but don't worry about defining them exactly.) Then use the Conversation Starters to talk about the lyrics. This is a fun way for your child to learn more about letters and words, and for both of you to learn more about each other.

Thanks for your time, and have fun!

Conversation Starters

1 After you have read the lyrics all the way through, reread the lyrics one line at a time and ask your child to choose the words that describe him or her. Ask why he or she chose each word. Add any words you think also describe your child and explain why. List the words on the back of this page.

2 Read the lyrics again, and ask your child to choose the words that describe you best. Ask why he or she chose each word. Add any words you think also describe you and explain why. List the words on the back of this page.

The ABCs of You

I think you're . . .
A-1, Grade A, beloved, beautiful,
Capable, caring, delightful, dependable,
Enjoyable, excellent, fascinating, fabulous,
A gift, a gem, genuinely generous,
Honest, highgrade, impressive, interesting,
A jewel, a jackpot, kindhearted, and a king,
Laudable, likeable, marvelous, magnificent,
Naturally nice . . .

One of a kind, pleasing, priceless,
Queenlike in quality, rare in radiance,
Scintillating, splendid, superb, sensational,
Trustworthy, talented, tender, and tasteful,
Unique, unprecedented, very very valuable,
Worthy, welcome, Xtraordinary, Xceptional,
Yes! Yes! Yes! You! You! You!
You're one in a zillion!

—Red Grammer*

* © 1991 Smilin' Atcha Music and Red and Kathy Grammer

In the space below, write (or help your child write) the words from the song that describe each of you.

Words from the Song That Describe the Child

....

....

....

....

....

....

....

Words from the Song That Describe the Adult

....

....

....

....

....

....

....

Comments

After you have completed this activity, each of you please sign your name and the date below. If you have any comments, please write them in the space provided.

....

....

....

....

Signatures

Date

....

Please have your child return this activity to school. Thank you.

New Year, New Semester

Before Sending Home the Activity

Have a class meeting to talk about how and when different cultures celebrate the New Year. Talk about why this is a special time for people to think about their achievements and to set goals for themselves. Encourage students to talk about what class accomplishments they are proud of, and then set some realistic goals for the rest of the school year. You might also give them an example of how people set personal goals by telling them about your own New Year's resolutions, when you were a child or now as an adult.

Follow-Up

Invite volunteers to show their pictures and explain their goals to their classmates.

New Year, New Semester

Dear Family Member or Family Friend,

This is a time when many cultures celebrate a New Year holiday. It is also the beginning of a new school semester. In class we have talked about what last semester was like, and what we want our class to be like for the new year.

This is also a good time for children to think about their own "new year." For this activity, please use the Conversation Starters to help your child think back to the beginning of school and remember what he or she especially wanted to learn. Talk about the progress that he or she has made, and help him or her set new (and realistic!) learning goals for the new semester. Then have your child draw a picture about one of these goals on the back of this page.

Thanks for your time, and have fun!

Conversation Starters

Here are some questions you might ask your child to get your conversation started. You can also make up different questions. You don't need to write down answers—I want children to practice their *talking* skills!

1 At the beginning of the school year, what did you look forward to learning?

(You may have to help your child remember back to the beginning of the school year—for example, was he or she looking forward to learning to read, learning to write, learning to count and add, learning about dinosaurs?)

2 How do you feel now about what you looked forward to learning? Did you find it interesting? Was there anything disappointing about learning it?

3 What would you like to learn during the rest of the school year?

(Now help your child set one or two learning goals for this semester. Make them simple, so your child will have a good chance of accomplishing them. On the back of this page, have your child draw a picture about one of these learning goals.)

In the space below, have your child draw a picture about one of his or her goals for this semester. If you'd like, help your child write a caption for the picture.

Comments

After you have completed this activity, each of you please sign your name and the date below. If you have any comments, please write them in the space provided.

Signatures   **Date**

Please have your child return this activity to school. Thank you.

Snowflakes

Before Sending Home the Activity

Have a snowflake-making session with your students, using photocopies of the diagram sheet included with this activity. If possible, give your students further opportunities to practice making snowflakes. (After the initial snowflake-making session, you might leave out a stack of snowflake sheets for students to use in their free time.) Have students make a class "snowstorm" by hanging up their snowflakes, and have a discussion about how the snowflakes are alike and different.

Follow-Up

Have students add their homemade snowflakes to the class snowstorm. You could then have partners describe to each other how they are like and different from family members, or the partners could make a list about each other's similarities and differences.

FOLD HERE
DOBLE EL PAPEL AQUI

Snowflakes

Dear Family Member or Family Friend,

In class we talk about how we are alike and how we are different. Like snowflakes, we are similar in many ways, but we are all different, too. Children who appreciate each other's similarities and differences can work well and learn well together.

This activity helps children develop such appreciation. Begin by making paper snowflakes together. (Instructions are on the next sheet.) Take turns telling how your snowflakes are alike and different. Then take turns naming some ways the two of you are alike and different. Your child may feel the comfort of being "the same as" you in some ways and the independence of being "different from" you, too.

Thanks for your time, and have fun!

Conversation Starters

On the attached pieces of paper, you will find a diagram showing you how to make snowflakes. Your child has already practiced this in school. Each of you make one snowflake, and then use the following suggestions to make comparisons.

1 Compare your snowflakes. Take turns telling each other how they are the same and how they are different.

2 Both of you think about some ways that you are similar to each other. Take turns naming these things. (For example, do you look alike? Do you act alike in some ways? Do you like the same books? TV shows? Foods? Sports?)

3 Now both of you think about some ways that you are different from each other. Take turns naming some of these things.

4 On the back of this page, help your child write some of the ideas you have talked about.

In the space below, help your child write lists of some of the ways you are alike and different.

Ways We Are Alike

....

....

....

....

....

....

....

Ways We Are Different

....

....

....

....

....

....

....

Comments

After you have completed this activity, each of you please sign your name and the date below. If you have any comments, please write them in the space provided.

....

....

....

....

Signatures   **Date**

....

Please have your child return this activity to school. Thank you.

Two Heads

Before Sending Home the Activity

Have the class do a partner activity the day you assign the Homeside Activity. During the wrap-up, spend time discussing what went well during partner work, what didn't go well, and how problems were solved by partners.

Explain that for the Homeside Activity, you want students to tell a parent or family friend about a favorite partner activity, either this one or a previous one; then give students a few minutes to think or talk about what activity to choose.

Follow-Up

Give students a chance to tell the class about doing the activity at home. Have partners show-and-tell one another about the picture of their adult working with a partner.

Two Heads

Dear Family Member or Family Friend,

In our classroom, students frequently work with partners. In many ways, "two heads are better than one" because students learn from each other and also learn to help each other. For young children, though, taking another person's thoughts and feelings into account can also be challenging.

For this activity, please use the Conversation Starters to talk with your child about his or her experiences of working with a partner. Then describe some of your own experiences working with a partner. On the back of this page, have your child draw a picture of you working with your partner.

Thanks for your time, and have fun!

Conversation Starters

Below are some questions and ideas to use in your conversation with your child. You can also make up different questions. You don't need to write down your child's answers—I want children to practice their *talking* skills!

1 Tell me about a time when you worked with a partner. What did you do with your partner? What did you enjoy most about working with a partner?

2 How did your partner help you learn? How did you help your partner learn?

3 Did you have any problems working with a partner? What did you do about this?

4 Now tell your child about a time you worked with another person to do a job. Explain how working with a partner helped you do your job. Describe any problems you had working with your partner and how you solved them. On the back of this page, have your child draw a picture of you working with your partner.

In the space below, have your child draw a picture of you working with your partner. If you'd like, help your child write a caption for the picture.

Comments

After you have completed this activity, each of you please sign your name and the date below. If you have any comments, please write them in the space provided.

Signatures   **Date**

Please have your child return this activity to school. Thank you.

Good Beginnings

Before Sending Home the Activity

Remind students that spring officially arrives at the end of March. Have a class discussion about spring, building on what students already know about the season. Talk with the class about the changes spring brings—longer daylight hours, the promise of warmer weather, blooming flowers and trees, the return of migrating and hibernating animals, the birth of baby animals, and so on. Talk with the class about how spring is a new beginning.

Follow-Up

Invite volunteers to tell the class about their good beginning pictures.

Good Beginnings

Dear Family Member or Family Friend,

People around the world look forward to the end of winter and the arrival of spring. In class, we talked about the many changes the season brings: longer daylight hours, warmer temperatures, blooming plants, and baby animals. We talked about how spring is a new beginning in many ways.

For this activity, please read aloud the poem "March" to your child. This poem points out some signs that spring is winning its chance to begin. Use the Conversation Starters to talk with your child about the poem and about a good beginning he or she has made.

Thanks for your time, and have fun!

March

A blue day,
a blue jay
and a good beginning.

One crow,
melting snow—
spring's winning!

—Elizabeth Coatsworth*

* From *The Random House Book of Poetry for Children*, selected by Jack Prelutsky, Random House, 1983.

Conversation Starters

Here are some questions you might ask your child to get your conversation started. You don't need to write answers—I want children to practice their *talking* skills!

1 What do you think of the poem?

(Also share your own reactions—for example, you could talk about what you both like or dislike about the poem, how the poem sounds, what it means, and so on.)

2 How do you feel about spring "winning" out over winter?

3 Now help your child think about a struggle he or she has (for example, learning a new skill, making a new friend, or solving a problem of some sort). Ask: What makes this thing hard for you? In what ways have you made a good beginning?

On the back of this page, have your child draw a picture about this "good beginning."

In the space below, have your child draw a picture of the "good beginning" he or she has made. If you'd like, help your child write a caption for the picture.

Comments

After you have completed this activity, each of you please sign your name and the date below. If you have any comments, please write them in the space provided.

Signatures   **Date**

Please have your child return this activity to school. Thank you.

Helping Chain

Before Sending Home the Activity

For each student, make two copies of the Helping Chain worksheet on colored paper; if possible, use two different colors, one for the child and one for the adult.

Make sure you do this activity in class before sending it home, so that students "get the hang of it." Have partners make Helping Chains, and decorate the classroom with them; you could personally add some links to the chain by expressing some of your own thoughts about students' helpfulness. (Students may want to make some links about how you help them, as well.)

Follow-Up

Have a whole-class conversation, asking students to volunteer what they learned about how their help is appreciated at home and how they liked (or disliked) this activity.

Helping Chain

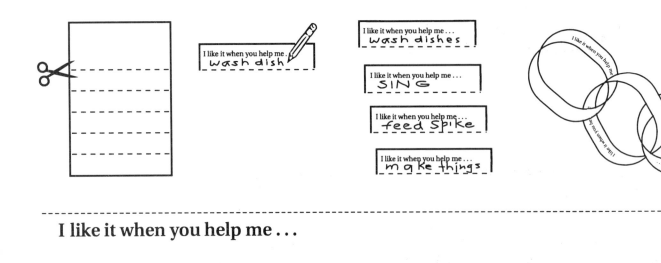

I like it when you help me . . .
wash dish

I like it when you help me . . .
wash dishes

I like it when you help me . . .
SING

I like it when you help me . . .
feed Spike

I like it when you help me . . .
make things

I like it when you help me . . .

I like it when you help me . . .

I like it when you help me . . .

I like it when you help me . . .

I like it when you help me . . .

Helping Chain

Dear Family Member or Family Friend,

As you know, in class we work to create a cooperative classroom community. We try to help each other and we try to show appreciation when others help us. One way we have done this is to make a class "Helping Chain." On the paper links that make up this chain, we write about how we like it when others help us.

For this activity, please make a "Helping Chain" with your child. Then on the back of this sheet have your child write a sentence about making the chain. (This activity involves a lot of writing, and you may help your child with the writing if you wish.) You may keep your Helping Chain at home, unless your child wants to bring it to school to show us. Please return this activity sheet with your comments.

Thanks for your time, and have fun!

Activity Directions

Here are some directions for making your home "Helping Chain." Please feel free to make the chain as long as you'd like and to involve other family members.

1 Each of you use one of the attached sheets of colored paper. (If additional family members want to help with the chain, share the colored paper with them or have them use any other colored or white paper you have at home.)

2 Take turns completing the sentences on your sheets of paper. For example, the adult's sheet might have such sentences as "I like it when you help me cook dinner" or "I like it when you help me by answering the phone for me." And the child's sheet might have such sentences as "I like it when you help me with my schoolwork" or "I like it when you help me learn to play softball."

3 Cut apart your strips along the dotted lines.

4 Use tape, staples, or glue to fasten the loops together like links in a chain, one through the other, alternating colors.

In the space below, have your child write a sentence saying what he or she liked (or disliked) about this activity. (You may help with the writing.)

....

....

....

....

....

....

....

....

....

....

....

Comments

After you have completed this activity, each of you please sign your name and the date below. If you have any comments, please write them in the space provided.

Signatures   **Date**

Please have your child return this activity to school. Thank you.

Accomplishments

Before Sending Home the Activity

Help students reflect on their accomplishments and the many activities they have engaged in during the past year. Have partners tell each other about their favorite things from the school year. Spend some time recalling the books you have read this year, and reread some class favorites. Have each student make a bookmark about a favorite story. If possible, laminate the bookmarks before sending them home.

Follow-Up

Have partners tell each other about their drawings and what they are proud of this year. Have students introduce their partners' drawings to the whole class.

Do some activities that encourage students to continue reading during the summer. For example, visit the public library, find out about summer reading programs, and help students obtain library cards if they have not done so already.

Accomplishments

Dear Family Member or Family Friend,

As the school year ends, our class has been reviewing the highlights of the year and all of the things we have accomplished. We have read many books this year, and we have enjoyed remembering our favorite stories. We even made bookmarks about the books we liked best. Children can use their bookmarks to mark their place in new favorite books they read this summer.

For this activity, please use the Conversation Starters to talk about your child's school year. Ask your child about the bookmark and the favorite book it shows. After your talk, your child can draw a picture about the school year on the back of this page.

Thanks for your time, and enjoy your talk!

Conversation Starters

Use the questions below to talk about your child's school year and favorite book. You can also make up other questions, if you'd like. Don't bother writing down the answers—I want children to practice their *talking* skills!

1 Tell me about your bookmark. What book does it show? What is the book about? What were some of your other favorite books this year?

2 What other things did you enjoy in school this year? What projects or subjects did you like best? Why?

3 What are you proud of learning or doing this year?

4 Now talk about some reasons you are proud of your child this year. Then have your child draw a picture about something he or she is proud of learning or doing this school year.

In the space below, have your child draw a picture of something he or she is proud of learning or doing this school year. If you'd like, help your child write a caption for the picture.

Comments

After you have completed this activity, each of you please sign your name and the date below. If you have any comments, please write them in the space provided.

Signatures

Date

Please have your child return this activity to school. Thank you.

Look What Happened!

Before Sending Home the Activity

This would be a good Homeside Activity to use in conjunction with an "end-the-year" activity.

Follow-Up

Invite volunteers to share their drawings with the rest of the class.

Look What Happened!

Dear Family Member or Family Friend,

June is a wonderful month! We're looking forward to summer vacation, and we're looking back at what we've learned during the school year. But this is sometimes a challenge for young children, who are just beginning to understand ideas of past, present, and future.

In this activity, you can help develop your child's sense of time by asking your child to share memories from the school year. You can also develop your child's sense of family history by sharing childhood memories from your own early years in school. Then have your child draw a picture, either about your memories of school or about his or her memories.

Thanks for your time, and have fun!

Conversation Starters

Here are some questions you might ask your child to get the conversation started. You can also make up different questions. You don't need to write down answers—I want children to practice their *talking* skills!

1 Tell me about things that happened in school this year. What kinds of things did you learn? What kinds of things did you do?

(Many children will want to talk about the present. To help your child think about the passage of time, try asking about the beginning of school, the changing seasons, or certain holidays.)

2 What did you enjoy learning this year?

3 Now tell what you remember best about your child's experience this year in school.

4 Tell your child memories of your experience in school when your were her or his age. On the back of this page, have your child draw a picture about the story you told or about the story your child told.

In the space below, have your child draw a picture showing something you talked about, either one of your child's memories or one of your own. If you'd like, help your child write a caption for the picture.

Comments

After you have completed this activity, each of you please sign your name and the date below. If you have any comments, please write them in the space provided.

Signatures

Date

Please have your child return this activity to school. Thank you.

Homeside Activities in Review

Before Sending Home the Activity

Have a class discussion about how Homeside Activities changed from the beginning to the end of the year. How did they get easier? How did they get harder? What did students do to help make the activities successful? What did parents or adult friends do to help make the activities successful? What were some favorite Homeside Activities? Explain the final Homeside Activity, and send home students' Homeside Activity folders along with it.

Follow-Up

Invite volunteers to tell about the Homeside Activities they created. Students might also enjoy making a Homeside Handbook for future students, with suggestions for making Homeside Activities successful. Or, they might enjoy compiling a class book about Homeside highlights that can be reproduced and taken home by students at the end of the school year so that they can share with each other the wisdom, experiences, and knowledge contributed by classmates' family members and friends. (If you reproduce actual finished Homeside Activities for this book, check with parents before sharing their contributions; an alternative would be to have students write about what they consider the Homeside Activity highlights and what they learned from them.)

Homeside Activities in Review

Dear Family Member or Family Friend,

I hope you have enjoyed doing Homeside Activities this year. Perhaps they gave you some insight into your child's school experience, and I'm sure your child has learned from your knowledge and experience while doing these activities. In class we have talked about what it has been like to do Homeside Activities, and which we liked best.

For this activity, please use the Conversation Starters to talk with your child about highlights of this year's Homeside Activities. Together, look over your child's folder of Homeside Activities from the year, and talk about which are your favorites. Then on the back of this page have your child write or draw about your conversation.

Thanks for your time, and have fun!

Conversation Starters

Below are some questions and ideas to use in your conversation with your child. You can also make up different questions. You don't need to write down your child's answers—I want children to practice their *talking* skills!

1 Together, look at the Homeside Activities your child has done this year. Tell each other what you liked about doing Homeside Activities.

2 Tell each other which were your favorite Homeside Activities. What did you like about these? Talk about the differences, if any, in your choices.

3 Ask your child to think of a topic or question that he or she would like to talk about for a Homeside Activity. Have a conversation about this topic.

4 On the back of this page, have your child write a sentence or two about this new Homeside Activity (or your child could draw a picture about it, instead).

In the space below, have your child write some sentences or draw a picture about the new Homeside Activity he or she created. If you'd like, help your child write a caption for the picture.

Comments

After you have completed this activity, each of you please sign your name and the date below. If you have any comments, please write them in the space provided.

Signatures   **Date**

Please have your child return this activity to school. Thank you.

Les presentamos las Actividades Familiares

Estimados padres, familiares o amigos:

Este año les voy a enviar a casa varias Actividades Familiares. Para llevar a cabo estas actividades, su hijo o su hija necesitará conversar con uno de sus padres o con otra persona mayor. Las conversaciones serán sobre temas relacionados con nuestro trabajo escolar.

Cada Actividad Familiar incluye una breve explicación de la actividad y algunas preguntas o ideas para ayudarles a realizar la actividad. La mayoría de estas actividades también le piden al niño o a la niña que haga un dibujo o que escriba algo sobre la conversación que haya tenido con usted.

No existe una única manera "correcta" de llevar a cabo estas actividades. Lo importante es que las disfruten juntos. Son una forma de reconocer y valorar lo mucho que usted le puede enseñar a su hijo o a su hija, al compartir sus experiencias y sus reflexiones con él o con ella.

Para esta primera Actividad Familiar, su hijo o su hija le mostrará una carpeta que ha hecho para guardar las Actividades Familiares. Haga el favor de utilizar las preguntas a continuación para conversar acerca de las Actividades Familiares. Luego pídale que haga un dibujo en el dorso de esta hoja sobre lo que han platicado.

Gracias por su atención y ¡que se diviertan!

Para iniciar el diálogo

Pídale a su hija o a su hijo que le muestre su carpeta para las Actividades Familiares. Luego utilice estas preguntas para conversar acerca de la carpeta y de las Actividades Familiares. No es necesario escribir las respuestas: lo importante aquí es que los niños desarrollen su capacidad de dialogar.

1 Cuéntame acerca de la carpeta y de cómo la diseñaste. ¿Cómo crees que van a ser las Actividades Familiares? ¿En qué manera serán distintas de otros tipos de tareas?

2 ¿De qué cosas te gusta conversar con las personas mayores? ¿Hay personas mayores en la escuela o en la comunidad con las que te gusta conversar? ¿Por qué te gustan esas pláticas?

3 Ahora cuéntele a su hija o a su hijo acerca de un pariente u otra persona mayor con la cual a usted le gustaba conversar cuando era menor. Pídale que haga un dibujo de usted cuando era menor, hablando con esa persona.

Pida a su hija o a su hijo que haga en este espacio un dibujo de usted cuando era menor, conversando con la persona mayor de la cual le habló. Luego anímele a escribir algo sobre el dibujo.

Comentarios

Después que hayan completado esta actividad, haga el favor cada uno de firmar y de escribir la fecha en el lugar indicado. Si Ud. quisiera hacer cualquier comentario, por favor escríbalo aquí.

Firmas

Fecha

Favor de enviar esta actividad de vuelta a la escuela con su hijo o con su hija. Muchísimas gracias.

¡Vamos a comenzar el año escolar!

Estimados padres, familiares o amigos:

El comienzo del año escolar conlleva mucho entusiasmo y a veces un poco de miedo para los niños. Por cierto, queremos aumentar su entusiasmo por lo que verán este año en la escuela. En la clase, hemos empezado a conocernos unos a otros. También hemos estado aprendiendo las reglas del salón, y conversando sobre las cosas que haremos este año.

Para esta actividad, quisiéramos pedirle que utilice las preguntas a continuación para ayudar a que su hijo o su hija le cuente de este nuevo año escolar. Es posible que ya le haya contado algunas de estas cosas, así que usted puede hacerle sus propias preguntas. Luego, pídale que haga un dibujo en el dorso de esta hoja de sí mismo o de sí misma aprendiendo algo que le interesa mucho. Con esta actividad, usted se enterará más sobre cómo es la clase, y yo podré conocer mejor a su hijo o a su hija.

Gracias por su atención y ¡diviértanse!

Para iniciar el diálogo

Éstas son preguntas que puede hacerle a su hijo o hija para comenzar la plática. También puede inventar sus propias preguntas. No es necesario escribir las respuestas: lo importante aquí es que los niños desarrollen su capacidad de dialogar.

1 ¿Cómo es tu salón de clase? ¿Qué te gusta del salón de clase? ¿Cuáles libros o materiales tienes ganas de utilizar?

2 Cuéntame de un amigo o de una amiga que has conocido en la clase. ¿Por qué son amigos? ¿Quién más podría ser un amigo o una amiga? ¿Por qué?

3 ¿Qué es lo que más te gusta de tu clase?

4 ¿Qué es lo que más quieres aprender este año? ¿Por qué piensas que eso sería interesante?

Pídale a su hijo o a su hija que haga un dibujo de sí mismo o de sí misma aprendiendo algo interesante en la escuela. Si quiere, puede ayudarle a escribir algo sobre el dibujo.

Comentarios

Después que hayan completado esta actividad, haga el favor cada uno de firmar y de escribir la fecha en el lugar indicado. Si Ud. quisiera hacer cualquier comentario, por favor escríbalo aquí.

Firmas   **Fecha**

Favor de enviar esta actividad de vuelta a la escuela con su hijo o con su hija. Muchísimas gracias.

Felipok
para Leo Tolstoy

Había una vez un niño llamado Felipe. Pero como era tan pequeño, todos le llamaban Felipok. Un día, cuando sus hermanos y hermanas estaban saliendo para la escuela, Felipok se puso su gorra, dispuesto a acompañarlos. Entonces su madre le dijo:

—¿A dónde vas, Felipok?

—A la escuela—dijo él.

—Todavía eres muy chiquito para ir a la escuela, Felipok—le dijo ella—. Debes quedarte en casa.

Los niños mayores se fueron a la escuela. Su padre había salido temprano por la mañana a trabajar en el bosque. Luego salió la madre, a limpiar la casa de una vecina rica. Felipok se quedó solo en la casa con su abuelita.

La abuela era muy ancianita. Como de costumbre, se quedó dormida en un rincón cerca de la estufa. Felipok se sintió solo y aburrido. Buscó su gorra y no la encontró. Así que se puso la gorra vieja de su padre y se fue solito camino a la escuela.

La escuela quedaba al otro lado del pueblo, cerca de la iglesia. Cuando Felipok bajó por su propia calle, los perros no lo molestaron, porque lo conocían. Pero más tarde, cuando pasaba en frente de casas desconocidas, muchos perros salieron de sus patios detrás de él. Uno de ellos era enorme. Todos los perros lo seguían, y ladraban. Felipok se echó a correr. Los perros lo perseguían, y ladraban más fuerte que nunca. Felipok lanzó un grito, tropezó y se cayó.

Vino un hombre que ahuyentó a los perros y le dijo al niño: —¿A dónde vas tan solito?

Felipok no le contestó, pero se echó a correr lo más rápido que pudo. Corrió hasta llegar a la escuela. No vio a nadie afuera, pero podía oír adentro las voces de los niños que estaban recitando sus lecciones. A Felipok le dio miedo. "¿Y qué si me corre el maestro?", pensó. No sabía qué hacer. Si regresaba a su casa, lo perseguirían los perros. Pero también le tenía miedo al maestro.

En eso pasó frente de la escuela una mujer llevando un balde de agua. Vio a Felipok y le dijo: —Los otros niños están adentro, aprendiendo. ¿Por qué estás aquí afuera, perdiendo el tiempo?

Felipok entró. Se quitó la capa en el pasillo y abrió la puerta del salón de clase. El salón estaba lleno de niños. Estaban hablando y gritando. El maestro tenía puesto una bufanda roja y caminaba entre las filas de mesas.

—¿Qué quieres tú? —le preguntó a Felipok en una voz muy seria.

El niño apretó su gorra y no dijo nada.

—¿Quién eres?

Felipok no contestó.

—¿Has perdido la lengua?

Ahora Felipok tenía tanto miedo que no podía decir ni media palabra.

—Regresa a tu casa si no quieres hablar —dijo el maestro.

A Felipok le hubiera gustado poder decir algo, pero tenía la garganta seca de miedo. Se quedó mirando al maestro y comenzó a llorar. Al maestro le dio pena. Lo abrazó y preguntó a los otros niños quién era él.

Los niños dijeron: —Es Felipok, el hermano menor de Kostushkin.

—Siempre quiere venir a la escuela.

—Su madre no lo dejó venir.

—Se vino de todos modos.

—En ese caso, chiquillo, anda a sentarte en esa banca, al lado de tu hermano. Voy a pedirle a tu madre que de ahora en adelante te deje venir a la escuela —le dijo el maestro.

Entonces comenzó a mostrarle a Felipok el abecedario, pero el niño ya se sabía todas las letras. Hasta podía leer un poco.

—Ahora dime cómo se deletrea tu nombre —dijo el maestro.

Tímido y con la mirada baja, Felipok deletreó su nombre rápidamente, como si tuviera miedo de que las letras se le iban a escapar si no se daba prisa.

La clase se echó a reir.

—¡Muy bien! —dijo el maestro—. Dime, ¿quién te enseñó todo esto?

Tomando más confianza, Felipok dijo: —Mi hermano Kostushka. Yo soy muy listo; aprendo muy rápido. ¡Soy muy inteligente!

El maestro se rió y le dijo: —No tengas tanta prisa de celebrarte a ti mismo. Primero estudia un poco más.

Y desde ese día, Felipok siempre fue a la escuela con sus hermanos y hermanas.

Felipok

Estimados padres, familiares o amigos:

Hoy estoy enviando a casa un cuento para que se lo lean a su hijo o a su hija. El cuento fue escrito por Leo Tolstoy, un gran novelista ruso. Mucha gente no sabe que Tolstoy escribió cuentos para niños, además de sus novelas para adultos.

Esta historia trata de un niño que quiere ir a la escuela, aún cuando alguna gente piensa que es demasiado joven. Es un buen cuento para el principio del año, cuando los niños se están acostumbrando a estar otra vez en la escuela.

Haga el favor de leer el cuento de Felipok a su hijo o a su hija. Luego utilice las preguntas que aparecen a continuación para ayudar a su hijo o a su hija a pensar sobre el cuento, y a pensar sobre lo que le gustaría aprender este año. Después que terminen su plática, pídale que haga un dibujo en el dorso de esta hoja sobre el cuento de Felipok.

Gracias por su atención y ¡diviértanse!

Para iniciar el diálogo

Aquí encontrará algunas preguntas que le puede hacer a su hijo o hija para empezar la plática. También puede inventar sus propias preguntas. No necesita escribir las respuestas: lo importante aquí es que los niños desarrollen su capacidad de dialogar.

1 ¿Qué te parece lo que hizo Felipok, de ir a la escuela sin el permiso de su mamá?

2 ¿Por qué crees que Felipok quería ir a la escuela? ¿Hay otras razónes que alguien pudiera tener para querer ir a la escuela?

3 Felipok podía deletrear su nombre muy bien. Hasta podía leer un poquito. ¿Cuáles son algunas de las cosas que tú puedes hacer bien en la escuela? (Como por ejemplo: decir el abecedario, leer los números, leer tu nombre, dibujar, cantar, jugar . . .)

4 Felipok quería aprender cosas nuevas en la escuela. ¿Cuáles son algunas de las cosas que tú quisieras aprender este año? ¿Por qué te gustaría aprender esas cosas?

5 Si gusta, cuéntele a su hijo o hija un recuerdo suyo de la escuela. ¿Tenía usted ganas de ir a la escuela, como Felipok? ¿O quizá tuvo un poco de miedo alguna vez? Luego invite a su hijo o a su hija a hacer un dibujo de Felipok en el dorso de esta hoja.

Invite a su hijo o a su hija a dibujar algo del cuento de Felipok. (Por ejemplo, podría dibujar a Felipok camino de la escuela o adentro de la escuela.) Si gusta, puede ayudarle a escribir algo sobre el dibujo.

Comentarios

Después que hayan completado esta actividad, haga el favor cada uno de firmar y de escribir la fecha en el lugar indicado. Si Ud. quisiera hacer cualquier comentario, por favor escríbalo aquí.

Firmas **Fecha**

Favor de enviar esta actividad de vuelta a la escuela con su hijo o con su hija. Muchísimas gracias.

Lo que me parece fácil

Estimados padres, familiares o amigos:

Tanto en la escuela como en la casa, los niños necesitan aprender muchas cosas nuevas. A veces se desaniman porque les es difícil hacer algo que a un hermano mayor, a una hermana mayor, o a una persona adulta le resulta fácil. Esperamos que esta actividad le ayude a su hija o a su hijo a ver que ya ha aprendido muchas cosas que antes le parecían difíciles, y que muchas de las cosas que ahora le parecen difíciles algún día le resultarán fáciles.

En el proceso de hacer listas, tanto de las cosas que son fáciles para cada uno de ustedes como de las que encuentran difíciles, su hijo o su hija se dará cuenta de que no son sólo los niños los que encuentran difíciles algunas cosas, sino también las personas mayores.

Gracias por su atención y ¡que se diviertan!

Para iniciar el diálogo

Aquí tiene algunas preguntas que puede utilizar para comenzar el diálogo. También puede inventar sus propias preguntas.

1 En el dorso de la hoja, escriba las respuestas que su hijo o su hija le dé a las siguientes preguntas.

- ¿Qué cosas puedes hacer con facilidad?
- ¿Qué cosas te son difíciles?

2 Cuéntele de algunas actividades que son fáciles para Ud. y de otras que son difíciles. Anótelas en el dorso de la hoja.

3 Lea la lista de "cosas fáciles" de su hija o de su hijo. Pregúntele si todas esas cosas le hubieran parecido fáciles hace un año. Cuéntele cómo fue que algunas de las cosas que ahora son fáciles para Ud., pudieron llegar a serlo.

4 Lea la lista de "cosas difíciles" de su hijo o de su hija, y pregúntele si piensa que algún día algunas de ellas le resultarán fáciles. Pregúntele cuáles de esas "cosas difíciles" le gustaría poder hacer y compartan algunas ideas sobre cómo podrían llegar a ser le más fáciles.

5 Cuéntele algunas ideas que tenga de cómo Ud. pudiera lograr que algo de su propia lista de cosas difíciles le resultara más fácil. Luego pregúntele si tiene algunas ideas que lo pudieran ayudar a Ud.

Lo que al niño o a la niña le parece fácil

Lo que al niño o a la niña le parece difícil

Lo que a la persona mayor le parece fácil

Lo que a la persona mayor le parece difícil

Comentarios

Después que hayan completado esta actividad, haga el favor cada uno de firmar y de escribir la fecha en el lugar indicado. Si Ud. quisiera hacer cualquier comentario, por favor escríbalo aquí.

Firmas

Fecha

Favor de enviar esta actividad de vuelta a la escuela con su hijo o con su hija. Muchísimas gracias.

El juego del abecedario

Estimados padres, familiares o amigos:

En clase, estamos llevando a cabo muchas actividades relacionadas con las letras del alfabeto. Cuando los niños comienzan a aprender el alfabeto, disfrutan al reconocer las letras a su alrededor. Esta actividad es un modo en que los niños pueden divertirse utilizando sus nuevos conocimientos.

Para esta actividad, haga el favor de seguir las indicaciones a continuación para jugar un juego de encontrar las letras con su hijo o con su hija. Pueden jugar este juego en casa o mientras pasean por el vecindario y también pueden incluir a los otros miembros de la familia. Haga el favor de jugar el juego juntos, más no de una manera competitiva (es importante que los niños sepan que las personas se ayudan unas a otras con el aprendizaje y que el aprender puede ser divertido).

Gracias por su atención y ¡que disfruten el juego!

Indicaciones para el juego

1 Con su hija o con su hijo, busquen la letra "A", ya sea dentro de la casa o afuera. Por ejemplo, pueden mirar libros, periódicos, los envases de las comidas, las etiquetas de la ropa, buzones, letreros, rótulos, carteles, etc. Luego busquen las siguientes letras del alfabeto en orden hasta que se cansen. (Recuerde que es un juego y queremos que sea divertido, no trabajoso.)

Para variar, pueden fijar un tiempo para encontrar tantos ejemplos de cada letra como puedan (por ejemplo, pueden fijar un lapso de cinco minutos).

2 Converse con su hijo o con su hija sobre el juego y ayúdele a escribir respuestas a las preguntas que encontrarán en el dorso de la hoja.

¿Cuáles fueron las letras más difíciles de encontrar? (Anoten todas las que quieran.)

_____

_____

_____

_____

_____

¿Cuáles fueron las letras más fáciles de encontrar? (Anoten todas las que quieran.)

_____

_____

_____

_____

_____

Comentarios

Después que hayan com-
pletado esta actividad,
haga el favor cada uno
de firmar y de escribir la
fecha en el lugar indicado.
Si Ud. quisiera hacer
cualquier comentario,
por favor escríbalo aquí.

Firmas   **Fecha**

_____   _____   _____

Favor de enviar esta actividad de vuelta a la escuela con su hijo o con su hija. Muchísimas gracias.

Un paseo por el vecindario

Estimados padres, familiares o amigos:

En la clase este año vamos a enfocarnos un poco en cómo el mirar las cosas desde otros puntos de vista nos ayuda a entender el mundo. Como todos vemos las cosas de maneras un poco distintas (nos gustan distintas canciones, distintos paisajes, distintos libros, distintas comidas) el entender y apreciar estas diferencias es parte importante del desarrollo.

Para esta actividad, usted y su hijo o su hija van a mirar una pequeña parte del mundo a través de los ojos del otro. Para hacer esto, primero darán un paseo corto por su vecindario. Al pasear juntos, observarán sus alrededores con mucha atención, pero sin hablar, señalar, ni comentar sobre lo que ven. Luego, cuando regresen a la casa, cada uno dirá cuáles fueron las cinco cosas más interesantes que vio y las anotarán en el lugar indicado.

Después que hayan escrito sus listas, podrán utilizar las preguntas que hemos provisto para comparar sus observaciones. Aun es posible que quieran volver a dar el paseo, para poder ver qué fue lo que observó la otra persona. Pídale a su hija o a su hijo que haga un dibujo en el dorso de esta hoja de algo interesante que uno de ustedes vio en el paseo.

Gracias por su atención y ¡diviértanse!

Las cosas más interesantes que vimos

Escriban aquí cinco de las cosas más interesantes que cada cual vio en el paseo. (Está bien si algunas de las cosas son las mismas.)

Desde el punto de vista del niño o de la niña

....
....
....
....
....

Desde el punto de vista de la persona mayor

....
....
....
....
....

Para iniciar el diálogo

1 Pregúntele a su hijo o a su hija en qué pensaba mientras caminaban. Luego cuéntele en qué pensaba Ud. ¿Cómo se parecen o se diferencian los pensamientos que tuvieron? ¿Por qué fue así?

2 ¿Cómo se sintieron al caminar sin poder conversar? ¿Por qué creen que se les pidió que no hablaran?

3 ¿Se interesan por las mismas cosas, o por cosas distintas? ¿Por qué? ¿Qué nos dice eso sobre la manera de mirar el mundo de cada persona?

Pídale a su hijo o a su hija que dibuje algo interesante que uno de ustedes vio en el paseo. Si quiere, puede ayudarle a escribir algo sobre su dibujo.

Comentarios

Después que hayan completado esta actividad, haga el favor cada uno de firmar y de escribir la fecha en el lugar indicado. Si Ud. quisiera hacer cualquier comentario, por favor escríbalo aquí.

Firmas   **Fecha**

Favor de enviar esta actividad de vuelta a la escuela con su hijo o con su hija. Muchísimas gracias.

Juguemos a agrupar

Estimados padres, familiares o amigos:

Nuestra clase está aprendiendo a ordenar y a agrupar. Estamos aprendiendo que los objetos pueden ser agrupados de muchas maneras distintas, según en qué nos fijamos y en los parecidos que buscamos.

Para esta actividad, Ud. y su hijo o su hija pensarán juntos en distintas maneras de agrupar diez objetos caseros. Haga el favor de utilizar las instrucciones que encontrará a continuación para ayudarles a jugar el juego. En esta actividad no se trata de obtener respuestas "correctas" o "incorrectas", sino de animar a su hija o a su hijo a pensar en varias maneras distintas de resolver el problema y de que lo pasen bien estando juntos.

Gracias por su atención y ¡que disfruten la actividad!

Instrucciones para el juego

1. Busquen diez objetos distintos que tengan en casa. (Por ejemplo: una manzana, un plátano, un envase de leche, un frijol, una caja de cereal, una toalla de papel, un carrito de juguete, un tubo de pasta de dientes, un sobre o un periódico.)

2. Piensen juntos en distintas formas de agrupar los objetos en dos grupos distintos. (Por ejemplo: objetos pequeños/objetos grandes; objetos comestibles/no comestibles; planos/no planos; brillantes/no brillantes; rojos/no rojos; que se guardan en una gaveta/que no se guardan en una gaveta; y así por el estilo.)

3. Escojan una manera de agrupar los objetos. Luego decidan juntos a cuál de los dos grupos pertenece cada objeto. Algunos de los objetos podrán resultar difíciles de clasificar. Por ejemplo: La pasta de dientes, ¿es comestible o no? El periódico, ¿es plano o no? El plátano maduro, ¿brilla o no brilla? Lo importante no es en cuál grupo deciden poner el objeto, sino el que conversen sobre sus razones por tomar una u otra decisión.

4. Invite a su hijo o a su hija a hacer un dibujo en el dorso de la hoja para mostrar cómo agruparon los objetos.

5. Luego pídale que escoja otra manera distinta de agrupar los objetos. Repitan juntos el paso nº 3. Vuelvan a repetir la actividad las veces que quieran, usando cada vez una manera distinta de agrupar los objetos. Si desean, pueden invitar a otros miembros de la familia a participar en el juego.

Invite a su hijo o a su hija a hacer un dibujo de los objetos ordenados en dos grupos distintos. Ayúdele a rotular cada grupo para mostrar cómo ordenaron los objetos.

Comentarios

Después que hayan completado esta actividad, haga el favor cada uno de firmar y de escribir la fecha en el lugar indicado. Si Ud. quisiera hacer cualquier comentario, por favor escríbalo aquí.

Firmas **Fecha**

Favor de enviar esta actividad de vuelta a la escuela con su hijo o con su hija. Muchísimas gracias.

La historia de mi nombre

**Estimados padres,
familiares o amigos:**

¿Conoce su hijo o su hija la historia de cómo le pusieron el nombre? En la clase, estaremos preparando una exhibición en la pared que muestre las historias de nuestros nombres.

Para esta Actividad Familiar, cuéntele a su hijo o a su hija todo lo que usted recuerde de cómo le pusieron su nombre. Las preguntas a continuación pueden ayudarle a recordar algunos de los detalles. Si su hijo o su hija ya conoce esta historia, permita que se la cuente a usted. Luego invítele a hacer un dibujo sobre la historia. Más tarde compartiremos algunas de estas historias en la clase.

Gracias por su atención y ¡diviértanse!

Preguntas para iniciar el diálogo

Si gusta, puede utilizar estas ideas para iniciar su relato.

1 Cuéntele a su hijo o a su hija todo lo que pueda recordar sobre cómo eligió su nombre.

¿Fue fácil escoger un nombre?

¿Cuánto tiempo le tomó?

¿Quiénes le dieron sugerencias?

¿Le dio a su hijo o a su hija el nombre de un pariente? ¿De algún amigo o amiga? ¿De alguien a quien usted admira?

¿Qué nombre le hubiera puesto a su hijo si hubiera sido una niña? ¿A su hija si hubiera sido un niño?

2 Cuéntele a su hijo o a su hija todo lo que usted sabe acerca de cómo le dieron a Ud. su nombre.

3 Cuéntele a su hijo o a su hija cómo Ud. se sentía con respecto a su propio nombre cuando era menor.

IDAD FAMILIAR

Invite a su hijo o a su hija a hacer un dibujo sobre la historia de su nombre. Si gusta, puede ayudarle a escribir algo sobre su dibujo.

Comentarios

Después que hayan completado esta actividad, haga el favor cada uno de firmar y de escribir la fecha en el lugar indicado. Si Ud. quisiera hacer cualquier comentario, por favor escríbalo aquí.

Firmas   **Fecha**

Favor de enviar esta actividad de vuelta a la escuela con su hijo o con su hija. Muchísimas gracias.

Dibujos que hablan

Estimados padres, familiares o amigos:

En la escuela, los niños con frecuencia hacen un dibujo para ilustrar un cuento. Para esta actividad, su hija o su hijo hará lo opuesto: inventará un cuento para acompañar un dibujo. Su hija o su hijo ha elegido un dibujo de una revista y lo utilizará para contarle un cuento. Si gusta, puede usar las preguntas que aparecen a continuación para ayudarle a comenzar.

El crear un cuento basado en un dibujo ayuda a mejorar las habilidades de observación y de comunicación de su hija o de su hijo. Pero no hay necesidad de tomar la actividad demasiado en serio: lo fundamental es ejercer la imaginación y divertirse.

Gracias por su atención y ¡que disfruten su plática!

Para iniciar el diálogo

Aquí tiene algunas preguntas e ideas para iniciar la conversación con su hija o con su hijo. También puede inventar sus propias preguntas. No es necesario escribir las respuestas: lo importante aquí es que los niños desarrollen su capacidad de dialogar.

1 Converse con su hija o con su hijo sobre la ilustración que ha traído de la escuela. Por ejemplo, podría preguntarle:

- ¿Por qué elegiste este dibujo?
- ¿Qué es lo que más te interesa de él?
- ¿Cómo te sientes cuando lo miras?

2 Cuéntele sus propias observaciones, pensamientos y sentimientos acerca del dibujo.

3 Pídale que invente un cuento acerca del dibujo. Puede ser un cuento sencillo. Por ejemplo, el cuento puede simplemente describir lo que piensa que está sucediendo en el dibujo.

4 Pídale que escriba un título para su cuento en el dorso de la hoja.

Pídale a su hija o a su hijo que escriba, en el espacio que sigue a continuación, un título para su cuento. (Si gusta, puede ayudarle con la escritura.)

El título de mi cuento:

_____

....

_____

_____

....

_____

_____

....

_____

Comentarios

Después que hayan com-
pletado esta actividad,
haga el favor cada uno
de firmar y de escribir la
fecha en el lugar indicado.
Si Ud. quisiera hacer
cualquier comentario,
por favor escríbalo aquí.

Firmas   Fecha

_____   _____   _____

Favor de enviar esta actividad de vuelta a la escuela con su hijo o con su hija. Muchísimas gracias.

Un abecedario para ti

Estimados padres, familiares o amigos:

Este poema está compuesto de palabras que comienzan con cada una de las letras del alfabeto. Haga el favor de leerlo con su hija o con su hijo. (Es probable que algunas de las palabras les sean desconocidas. Quizá querrán explorar su significado a fondo más tarde, pero por ahora no se preocupen de obtener una definición exacta.) Luego utilicen las indicaciones y las preguntas a continuación para conversar acerca del poema. Esta actividad es una forma divertida en que su hija o su hijo puede aprender más acerca de las letras y las palabras, y en que cada uno pueda aprender más acerca del otro.

Gracias por su atención y ¡diviértanse!

Para iniciar el diálogo

1 Lean el poema entero en voz alta. Luego pida a su hija o a su hijo que escoja las palabras que describan quién es él o quién es ella. Pídale que explique por qué escogió cada palabra. Añada cualquier palabra que usted piense que lo describa a él o la describa a ella, y explíquele por qué. Hagan una lista con estas palabras en el dorso de la hoja.

2 Lea el poema otra vez y pida a su hija o a su hijo que escoja palabras que describan quién es usted. Pregúntele por qué eligió cada palabra. Añada cualquier palabra que usted piense que lo describa a si mismo o la describa a si misma, y explíquele por qué. Hagan una lista con estas palabras en el dorso de la hoja.

Tu abecedario

Te veo
amable, agradable
amante de la bondad
bienandante
capaz y constante
de mucha chispa
decente
ejemplar y eminente
fuerte, fascinante
genial y gentil
de mucha honestidad
interesante e impresionante
¡una joya!
laudable y loable
llenas la vida de maravilla
muy naturalmente noble
¡ñeque!
optimista, paciente y perspicaz
¡cómo te quiero!
radiante, razonable, sensible
siempre en solidaridad
tenaz, tenaz, tenaz
tu presencia es única
y útil
eres valiente y vivaz
(e)xtraordinariamente
(e)xcelente
y,
¡ya sé!
un zafiro que brilla
con amor y alegría
brindando cariño
apoyo
y paz.

—por Alma Flor Ada y Rosa Zubizarreta
inspirado en un poema de Red Grammer

En el espacio a continuación, escriba (o ayude a que su hija o su hijo escriba) las palabras del poema que describen a cada uno de ustedes.

Las palabras del poema que describen al niño o a la niña

Las palabras del poema que describen a la persona mayor

Comentarios

Despúes que hayan completado esta actividad, haga el favor cada uno de firmar y de escribir la fecha en el lugar indicado. Si Ud. quisiera hacer cualquier comentario, por favor escríbalo aquí.

Firmas

Fecha

Favor de enviar esta actividad de vuelta a la escuela con su hijo o con su hija. Muchísimas gracias.

Año nuevo, semestre nuevo

Estimados padres, familiares o amigos:

Ésta es una época del año en que muchas culturas celebran el Año Nuevo. También es el comienzo de un nuevo semestre escolar. En la clase hemos hablado sobre el semestre pasado y de cómo queremos que sea nuestra clase este año.

Éste también es buen momento para que los niños reflexionen sobre su propio "año nuevo". Para esta actividad familiar, haga el favor de utilizar las preguntas a continuación para ayudarle a su hijo o a su hija a recordar su comienzo en la escuela, y qué era lo que tenía más ganas de aprender. Conversen sobre cómo ha progresado y ayúdele a proponerse nuevos objetivos de aprendizaje para el próximo semestre.

Luego invite a su hija o a su hijo a hacer un dibujo en el dorso de esta hoja sobre una de sus propias metas.

Gracias por su atención y ¡diviértanse!

Para iniciar el diálogo

Aquí tiene algunas preguntas que puede hacerle a su hijo o a su hija para iniciar el diálogo. También puede inventar otras preguntas. No es necesario escribir las respuestas: lo importante aquí es que los niños desarrollen su capacidad de dialogar.

1 Pídale a su hijo o a su hija que le hable de lo que tenía más ganas de aprender al comienzo del año escolar.

(Quizá tenga que ayudarle a recordar el comienzo del año escolar. Por ejemplo: pregúntele si tenía ganas de aprender a leer o a escribir, a contar y a sumar o de aprender sobre los dinosaurios.)

2 Pregúntele a su hijo o a su hija cómo se siente ahora ante aquello que deseaba aprender.

¿Qué es lo que has aprendido?

¿Te interesa seguir aprendiendo más?

¿Has tenido alguna desilusión mientras intentabas aprender algo?

3 Pregúntele qué quiere aprender durante el resto del año escolar.

Ayúdele a proponerse uno o dos objetivos para este semestre. (Es importante que sean objetivos sencillos, para que, con un poco de esfuerzo, los pueda cumplir.) Pídale que dibuje en el dorso de esta hoja uno de estos objetivos.

Pídale a su hijo o a su hija que haga un dibujo sobre alguno de sus objetivos para este nuevo semestre. Si gusta, puede ayudarle a escribir algo sobre su dibujo.

Comentarios

Después que hayan completado esta actividad, haga el favor cada uno de firmar y de escribir la fecha en el lugar indicado. Si Ud. quisiera hacer cualquier comentario, por favor escríbalo aquí.

....

....

....

....

....

Firmas　　　　　　　　　　　　　　　　　　　　　　　　**Fecha**

Favor de enviar esta actividad de vuelta a la escuela con su hijo o con su hija. Muchísimas gracias.

Copos de nieve

Estimados padres, familiares o amigos:

En la clase hemos conversado sobre el hecho de que todos somos semejantes y a la vez diferentes. Como los copos de nieve, en muchas formas nos parecemos, pero también somos distintos. Los niños que aprecian las semejanzas y respetan las diferencias que tienen entre sí pueden trabajar y aprender bien juntos.

Esta actividad ayuda a los niños a desarrollar este tipo de comprensión. Empiecen por hacer juntos copos de nieve siguiendo las instrucciones de la otra hoja. Luego cada cual dirá en qué se parecen y en qué se diferencian sus copos de nieve. Cuando cada persona haya tenido varios turnos, pasen a describir cuáles son algunas de las semejanzas y de las diferencias entre ustedes. Su hijo o su hija se sentirá apoyado al ver que "se parece" a usted en algunas cosas y se sentirá independiente al ver que en otras es "diferente".

Gracias por su atención y !diviértanse!

Para iniciar el diálogo

En las hojas que se incluyen, encontrará un diagrama que muestra cómo hacer los copos de nieve. Su hijo o su hija ya habrá practicado esta actividad en la clase. Cada uno de ustedes hará un copo de nieve. Luego podrá utilizar estas sugerencias para hacer las comparaciones.

1 Comparen los copos de nieve. Túrnense para decir en qué se parecen y en qué se diferencian.

2 Piensen en algunas formas en que ustedes dos se parecen. Túrnense para nombrarlas. (Por ejemplo: ¿Se parecen físicamente? ¿Actúan en forma parecida? ¿Les gustan los mismos libros? ¿Los mismos programas de televisión? ¿Las mismas comidas? ¿Deportes?)

3 Ahora piensen ambos en qué son distintos. Túrnense para hablar de las diferencias entre ustedes.

4 Ayúdele a su hijo o a su hija a escribir, en el dorso de esta hoja, algunas de las cosas de las cuales han hablado.

Ayude a su hijo o a su hija a escribir listas de las semejanzas y de las diferencias entre ustedes.

En qué nos parecemos

En qué somos diferentes

....

Comentarios
....

Después que hayan completado esta actividad, haga el favor cada uno de firmar y de escribir la fecha en el lugar indicado. Si Ud. quisiera hacer cualquier comentario, por favor escríbalo aquí.

Firmas

Fecha

Favor de enviar esta actividad de vuelta a la escuela con su hijo o con su hija. Muchísimas gracias.

Dos cabezas

Estimados padres, familiares o amigos:

En nuestra clase, los alumnos frecuentemente trabajan en parejas. En inglés hay un dicho: "dos cabezas piensan mejor que una" ya que al trabajar en conjunto, los alumnos aprenden unos de otros y también aprenden cómo ayudarse mutuamente. Pero a veces les es difícil a los niños pequeños el aprender a considerar los pensamientos y los sentimientos de los demás.

Para esta actividad, haga el favor de utilizar las preguntas que aparecen a continuación para conversar con su hija o con su hijo acerca de las experiencias que ella o que él ha tenido trabajando en parejas. Luego, cuéntele sobre algunas de las experiencias que Ud. ha tenido trabajando con alguien. Pídale que haga un dibujo en el dorso de la hoja que lo muestre a Ud. trabajando con un compañero o con una compañera.

Gracias por su atención y ¡que se diviertan!

Para iniciar el diálogo

Aquí le ofrecemos algunas preguntas e ideas que puede utilizar en la conversación con su hija o con su hijo. También puede inventar, si gusta, sus propias preguntas. No es necesario escribir las respuestas: lo importante aquí es que los niños desarrollen su capacidad de dialogar.

1 Cuéntame de alguna vez en que trabajaste en pareja. ¿Qué hiciste con tu compañero o con tu compañera? ¿Qué fue lo que más te gustó de trabajar en pareja?

2 ¿De qué manera te ayudó a aprender tu compañero o tu compañera? ¿Cómo le ayudaste tú a aprender?

3 ¿Tuviste algún problema al trabajar con tu compañero o con tu compañera? ¿Qué hicieron para resolverlo?

4 Ahora cuéntele acerca de alguna vez en que Ud. trabajó con otra persona. Explíquele de qué manera el trabajar con alguien le ayudó a realizar el trabajo. Hable sobre cualquier dificultad que tuvo al trabajar en pareja y de cómo lo resolvió. Pídale que haga un dibujo, en el dorso de esta hoja, que lo muestre a Ud. trabajando con un compañero o con una compañera.

Pídale a su hija o a su hijo que haga un dibujo que lo muestre a Ud. trabajando con alguien. Si gusta, puede ayudarle a escribir algo sobre su dibujo.

Comentarios

Después que hayan completado esta actividad, haga el favor cada uno de firmar y de escribir la fecha en el lugar indicado. Si Ud. quisiera hacer cualquier comentario, por favor escríbalo aquí.

Firmas
Fecha

Favor de enviar esta actividad de vuelta a la escuela con su hijo o con su hija. Muchísimas gracias.

Los buenos comienzos

Estimados padres, familiares o amigos:

En muchas partes del mundo se espera con entusiasmo el final del invierno y el comienzo de la primavera. En la clase hemos hablado de la primavera y de los muchos cambios que trae: los días más largos, el clima más cálido, las plantas que florecen y los animales recién nacidos. Hablamos de la primavera como un nuevo comienzo.

Lea el poema "Marzo" en voz alta a su hijo o a su hija. Este poema describe algunas de las señas de que la primavera está "ganando la oportunidad" de establecer un nuevo comienzo. Utilice las preguntas que aparecen a continuación para hablar con su hijo o con su hija sobre el poema, y ayúdele a celebrar sus propios buenos comienzos.

Gracias por su atención y ¡diviértanse!

Marzo

Azul está el cielo—
un azulejo en vuelo:
algo nuevo está comenzando.

Un cuervo grita:
—¡Que la nieve se derrita!
la primavera está ganando.

—Elizabeth Coatsworth*
(traducido por Rosa Zubizarreta)

Para iniciar el diálogo

Aquí tiene algunas preguntas que puede hacerle a su hijo o su hija para iniciar el diálogo. También puede inventar sus propias preguntas. No es necesario escribir las respuestas: lo importante es que los niños desarrollen su capacidad de dialogar.

1 ¿Qué piensas del poema? (También comparta sus propias impresiones. Por ejemplo, pueden conversar de lo que les gusta o lo que no les gusta del poema, de cómo es el sonido del poema, de lo que significa, y así por el estilo.)

2 ¿Cómo te sientes al saber que la primavera está "ganándole" al invierno?

3 Ayude a su hija o a su hijo a pensar en alguna dificultad que está enfrentando en su vida. (Podría ser el esfuerzo necesario para aprender algo nuevo, para adquirir una nueva habilidad, para hacer un nuevo amigo, o para resolver algún tipo de problema.) Pregúntele:

- ¿Qué hace que esto sea difícil para ti?
- ¿Qué buen comienzo has hecho ya?

Pídale a su hija o a su hijo que haga un dibujo en el revés de la hoja sobre su "buen comienzo."

* From *The Random House Book of Poetry for Children*, selected by Jack Prelutsky, Random House, 1983.

Invite a su hijo o a su hija a hacer un dibujo del buen comienzo que ya ha logrado.
Si gusta, puede ayudarle a escribir algo sobre su dibujo.

Comentarios

Después que hayan completado esta actividad, haga el favor cada uno de firmar y de escribir la fecha en el lugar indicado. Si Ud. quisiera hacer cualquier comentario, por favor escríbalo aquí.

Firmas

Fecha

Favor de enviar esta actividad de vuelta a la escuela con su hijo o con su hija. Muchísimas gracias.

Una cadena de apoyo

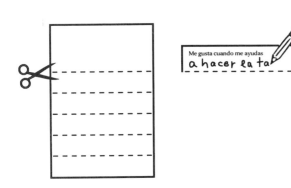

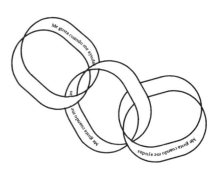

Me gusta cuando me ayudas . . .

Me gusta cuando me ayudas . . .

Me gusta cuando me ayudas . . .

Me gusta cuando me ayudas . . .

Me gusta cuando me ayudas . . .

CADENA DE APOYO

Una cadena de apoyo

Estimados padres, familiares o amigos:

Ya saben que en la clase nos esforzamos por crear una comunidad cooperativa. Tratamos de ayudarnos unos a otros y procuramos mostrar aprecio por la ayuda que recibimos de los demás. Una manera en la cual hemos reforzado estos principios es que hemos creado una "Cadena de apoyo" en la clase. En los eslabones de papel que forman esta cadena, hemos escrito cómo nos sentimos cuando otros nos ayudan.

Para esta actividad, hagan el favor de construir una "Cadena de apoyo" juntos. Luego pídale a su hijo o a su hija que escriba una oración en el dorso de esta hoja sobre cómo fue el crear la cadena. (Para completar esta actividad necesitarán escribir bastante. Si desea, puede ayudarle a su hijo o a su hija con la escritura.) Pueden quedarse con la "Cadena de apoyo" en casa, al menos que su hijo o su hija quiere traer la cadena a la escuela para mostrárnosla. Haga el favor de devolver esta hoja a la escuela junto con sus comentarios.

Muchas gracias por su atención y ¡diviértanse!

Instrucciones

Aquí tienen las instrucciones para construir la "Cadena de apoyo". Por favor siéntanse en libertad de hacer la cadena del largo que quieran y de incluir en su fabricación a los otros miembros de la familia.

1 Cada uno de ustedes utilizará una de las hojas de papel de color que se incluyen con la actividad. (Si hay otros miembros de la familia que quieren participar, pueden compartir las hojas con ellos o utilizar otras hojas de papel que tengan en casa.)

2 Dense turnos para completar las oraciones que tienen en sus hojas. Por ejemplo, la hoja de la persona mayor podría tener oraciones como las siguientes: "Me gusta cuando me ayudas a cocinar la comida" o "Me gusta cuando me ayudas y contestas el teléfono". La hoja del alumno podría tener oraciones tal como: "Me gusta cuando me ayudas con mis tareas" o "Me gusta cuando me ayudas a aprender un deporte".

3 Recorten sus tiras de papel por las líneas indicadas.

4 Usen pegamento o cinta adhesiva para juntar las tiras y formar los eslabones de la cadena, alternando los colores y pasando cada eslabón por el eslabón previo.

Invite a su hijo o a su hija a que escriba una oración en este espacio sobre lo que le gustó (o lo que no le gustó) de la actividad. (Si desea, puede ayudarle con la escritura.)

Comentarios

Después que hayan completado esta actividad, haga el favor cada uno de firmar y de escribir la fecha en el lugar indicado. Si Ud. quisiera hacer cualquier comentario, por favor escríbalo aquí.

Firmas

Fecha

Favor de enviar esta actividad de vuelta a la escuela con su hijo o con su hija. Muchísimas gracias.

Nuestros logros

Estimados padres, familiares o amigos:

Ya que termina el año escolar, en la clase estamos repasando los acontecimientos del año y todo lo que hemos logrado. Hemos leído muchos libros este año y hemos disfrutado al recordar nuestros cuentos favoritos. También hemos hecho señaladores, que hemos ilustrado con temas de los libros que más nos han gustado. Los niños pueden utilizar su señalador para marcar su lugar en los libros nuevos que leerán con gusto este verano.

Para esta actividad, haga el favor de utilizar las preguntas que encontrará a continuación para conversar acerca del año escolar de su hija o de su hijo. Pregúntele acerca de su señalador y del libro favorito al que se refiere. Después de su conversación, pida a su hija o a su hijo que haga un dibujo en el dorso de esta hoja acerca de su año escolar.

Gracias por su atención y ¡que disfruten su conversación!

Para iniciar el diálogo

Utilice estas preguntas para conversar con su hija o con su hijo acerca de este año escolar y de su libro favorito. También puede inventar sus propios preguntas, si lo desea. No se preocupe de escribir las respuestas—lo importante aquí es que los niños desarrollen la habilidad de dialogar.

1 Cuéntame algo acerca de tu señalador. ¿A qué libro se refiere? ¿De qué se trata ese libro? ¿Cuáles fueron algunos de tus otros libros favoritos este año?

2 ¿Qué otras cosas disfrutaste en la escuela este año? ¿Qué proyectos o materias te gustaron más? ¿Por qué?

3 ¿Hay algo que aprendiste o que hiciste que te da una satisfacción especial?

4 Conversen acerca de algunas de las formas en que su hijo o su hija le ha dado mucha alegría a Ud. este año. Luego pídale que haga un dibujo acerca de algo que ha hecho este año escolar que lo ayuda a sentirse satisfecho de sí mismo o satisfecha de sí misma.

Invite a su hijo o a su hija a hacer un dibujo en el espacio a continuación sobre algo que haya hecho este año escolar de lo cual se siente muy satisfecho o muy satisfecha. Si gusta, puede ayudarle a escribir algo sobre su dibujo.

Comentarios

Después que hayan completado esta actividad, haga el favor cada uno de firmar y de escribir la fecha en el lugar indicado. Si Ud. quisiera hacer cualquier comentario, por favor escríbalo aquí.

Firmas

Fecha

Favor de enviar esta actividad de vuelta a la escuela con su hijo o con su hija. Muchísimas gracias.

¡Mira todo lo que sucedió!

Estimados padres, familiares o amigos:

Junio es un mes maravilloso. Estamos esperando las vacaciones de verano con entusiasmo, y también estamos recordando el año escolar y recapacitando en todo lo que hemos aprendido a lo largo de él. Pero a veces esto les es un poco difícil para los niños, que recién están comenzando a entender los conceptos del presente, el futuro y el pasado.

En esta actividad, puede ayudar a desarrollar el sentido del tiempo de su hijo o de su hija, pidiéndole que comparta algunos de sus recuerdos sobre este año escolar. También puede ayudarle a desarrollar su sentido de historia familiar, al compartir con él o con ella algunos de sus propios recuerdos de sus primeros años de escuela. Luego invítele a hacer un dibujo, ya sea de los recuerdos que él o que ella tenga sobre este año escolar, o de los que usted le haya relatado.

Gracias por su atención y ¡diviértanse!

Para iniciar el diálogo

Puede utilizar estas preguntas para iniciar el diálogo con su hijo o con su hija. También puede inventar otras. No es necesario anotar las respuestas, ya que lo importante aquí es que los niños desarrollen su capacidad de dialogar.

1 Cuéntame algunas de las cosas que sucedieron en la escuela este año.

(Muchas veces los niños querrán hablar sobre el presente. Para ayudarle a su hijo o a su hija a pensar sobre el paso del tiempo, intente hacerle preguntas sobre el comienzo del año, las distintas estaciones o los días feriados que hayan celebrado.)

2 ¿Qué te gustó aprender este año?

3 Ahora cuéntele lo que usted más recuerda de este año escolar.

4 Cuéntele los recuerdos que tiene de su propia experiencia escolar cuando tenía la edad de él o de ella. Pídale que haga un dibujo en el dorso de esta hoja sobre lo que usted le ha relatado, o sobre lo que él o ella le ha contado a Ud.

Pídale a su hijo o a su hija que haga un dibujo sobre algo de lo que han hablado. Puede dibujar uno de sus propios recuerdos o algo que usted le haya contado.

Comentarios

Después que hayan completado esta actividad, haga el favor cada uno de firmar y de escribir la fecha en el lugar indicado. Si Ud. quisiera hacer cualquier comentario, por favor escríbalo aquí.

Firmas   **Fecha**

Favor de enviar esta actividad de vuelta a la escuela con su hijo o con su hija. Muchísimas gracias.

Repasemos las Actividades Familiares

Estimados padres, familiares o amigos:

Espero que este año hayan disfrutado las Actividades Familiares. Esperamos que le hayan ayudado a comprender mejor la experiencia escolar de su hija o de su hijo. Lo cierto es que, al realizar estas actividades, ella o él ha aprendido mucho a raíz del conocimiento y de la experiencia de Ud.

En la clase, hemos conversado sobre cómo nos fue con las Actividades Familiares, y cuáles de ellas nos han gustado más. Para esta actividad, haga el favor de utilizar las preguntas a continuación para conversar con su hija o con su hijo acerca de algunos momentos especiales que hayan tenido este año al compartir las Actividades Familiares.

Repasen juntos el contenido de la carpeta de Actividades familiares, y conversen acerca de cuáles actividades fueron sus favoritas. Luego pida a su hijo o a su hija que haga un dibujo o que escriba algo en el dorso de la hoja acerca de su conversación.

Gracias por su atención y ¡que se diviertan!

Para iniciar el diálogo

Aquí tiene algunas preguntas e ideas que puede usar para conversar con su hija o con su hijo. También puede inventar sus propias preguntas. No es necesario escribir las respuestas: lo importante aquí es que los niños tengan la oportunidad de desarrollar su capacidad de dialogar.

1. Revisen juntos las Actividades Familiares que su hija o que su hijo ha completado este año. Hablen de qué es lo que les ha gustado de las Actividades Familiares.

2. Conversen sobre cuáles fueron sus Actividades Familiares preferidas. ¿Qué fue lo que les gustó de esas actividades? Si han elegido actividades distintas, conversen sobre las diferencias entre sus selecciones.

3. Pida a su hija o a su hijo que piense sobre un tema o una pregunta que le gustaría explorar en una Actividad Familiar. Conversen sobre ese tema.

4. Pida a su hija o a su hijo que escriba unas cuantas oraciones en el dorso de esta hoja acerca de esta nueva Actividad Familiar. (Si prefiere, puede hacer un dibujo acerca de la actividad.)

Pida a su hija o a su hijo que escriba algunas oraciones o que haga un dibujo en el espacio a continuación sobre la nueva Actividad Familiar que acaban de crear.

Comentarios

Después que hayan completado esta actividad, haga el favor cada uno de firmar y de escribir la fecha en el lugar indicado. Si Ud. tiene cualquier comentario, por favor escríbalo en este espacio.

Firmas

Fecha

Favor de enviar esta actividad de vuelta a la escuela con su hijo o con su hija. Muchísimas gracias.

▶ AVAILABLE FROM DEVELOPMENTAL STUDIES CENTER

Homeside Activities Books (Grades K–5). Six separate collections of activities that help teachers, parents, and children communicate. Each collection has an introductory overview, 18 reproducible take-home activities in English and Spanish, and teacher suggestions for integrating the activities into the life of the classroom.

Homeside Activities Videotape. A 12-minute video that can be used at parent gatherings and staff meetings as an overview of a program of Homeside Activities. Documentary footage shows a range of classroom grades and home settings.

At Home in Our Schools. A 136-page guide to whole-school activities that help educators and parents create caring school communities. Ideas about leadership, step-by-step guidelines for 15 activities, and reproducible planning resources and suggestions for teachers.

At Home in Our Schools Videotape. A 12-minute video to use in staff meetings and PTO/parent gatherings to create support for a program of whole-school activities that build community. Documentary footage of diverse schools using community-building activities.

Reading, Thinking & Caring: Literature-based Reading (Grades K–3). A children's literature program to help students love to read, think deeply and critically, and care about how they treat themselves and others. Teaching units are available for over 80 classic, contemporary, and multicultural titles. Each 3- to 10-day unit includes a take-home activity in English and Spanish to involve parents in their children's life at school. Complete grade-level sets, individual teaching units, and accompanying trade books all available.

Reading for Real: Literature-based Reading (Grades 4–8). A literature-based program to engage students' consciences while providing reading and writing experiences that are engaging for young people. Teaching units are available for over 100 classic, contemporary, and multicultural titles. Each 1- to 3-week unit includes a take-home activity to involve parents in their children's life at school. Teachers report that this program engages even reluctant readers and builds community in the classroom. Complete grade-level sets, individual teaching units, orientation video-tape, and accompanying trade books all available.

Number Power: Teacher Resource Books (Grades K–6). Seven separate *Number Power* books (one per grade) provide three replacement units (8–12 lessons per unit) that foster students' mathematical and social development. Students collaboratively investigate problems, develop their number sense, enhance their mathematical reasoning and communication skills, and learn to work together effectively.

Number Power: Teacher Resource Packages (Grades K–6). Grade-level boxed collections of ready-to-use transparencies, die-cut manipulatives, blackline masters, and pads of group record sheets.

▶ COMING SOON FROM DEVELOPMENTAL STUDIES CENTER

Ideas for a Buddies Program at Your School. Whether for a whole school program of cross-grade buddies or for two cooperating classrooms, this book is a practical guide that draws on the experiences of teachers from Child Development Project schools across the country.

Using Class Meetings to Build Caring and Responsible Relationships. Guidelines for eight different kinds of class meetings (at two different levels: K–3 and 4–6); tips on getting started and logistics.

Classroom as Community: Collaborative Learning in Action. Visits to collaborative classrooms in American pilot schools of the Child Development Project showcase thoughtful teachers and the various ways they use CDP cooperative learning to build classroom communities.

Structuring a Collaborative Classroom. An in-depth look at CDP cooperative learning that includes sample step-by-step lessons, strategic structures, and an in-depth case study of one classroom where teacher and students wrestle with the day-to-day realities of using cooperative learning to build a collaborative classroom.

▶ FOR ORDERING INFORMATION CALL 1-800-666-7270 OR 510-533-0213, PUBLICATIONS DEPARTMENT